When Harry Met Sally...

CASTLE ROCK ENTERTAINMENT IN ASSOCIATION WITH NELSON ENTERTAINMENT PRESENTS A ROB REINER FILM BILLY CRYSTAL   MEG RYAN "WHEN HARRY MET SALLY..." CARRIE FISHER   BRUNO KIRBY EDITED BY ROBERT LEIGHTON PRODUCTION DESIGNER JANE MUSKY DIRECTOR OF PHOTOGRAPHY BARRY SONNENFELD MUSIC ADAPTED AND ARRANGED BY MARC SHAIMAN PRODUCED BY ROB REINER AND ANDREW SCHEINMAN WRITTEN BY NORA EPHRON DIRECTED BY ROB REINER

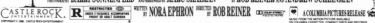

When Harry Met Sally...

When Harry Met Sally...

NORA EPHRON

ALFRED A. KNOPF NEW YORK 1990

THIS IS A BORZOI BOOK
PUBLISHED BY ALFRED A. KNOPF, INC.

Library of Congress Cataloging-in-Publication Data
Ephron, Nora.
When Harry met Sally— / Nora Ephron.—1st ed.
p. cm.
ISBN 0-679-72903-8
I. Title.
PN1997.W466   1990
791.43'72—dc20   89-43595
                                              CIP

Manufactured in the United States of America
First Edition

For Nick

Introduction

by Nora Ephron

This screenplay has my name on it, but it was very much a collaboration, and before I write a word about the movie itself, I want to write about how it got started. It began in October 1984, when I got a call from my agent that Rob Reiner and his producing partner Andrew Scheinman wanted to have lunch to discuss a project. So we had a lunch, and they told me about an idea they had for a movie about a lawyer. I've forgotten the details. The point is, it didn't interest me at all, and I couldn't imagine why they'd thought of me in connection with it. I remember being slightly perplexed about whether to say straight off that the idea didn't interest me or whether to play along for an hour so as not to have that horrible awkwardness that can happen when the meeting is over but the lunch must go on. I decided on the former; and we then spent the rest of the lunch talking about ourselves. Well, that isn't entirely true: we spent the rest of the lunch talking about Rob and Andy. Rob was divorced, and Andy was a bachelor—and they were both extremely funny and candid about their lives as single men in Los Angeles. When the lunch ended, we still didn't have an idea for a movie; but we decided to meet again the next time they were in New York.

And so, a month later, we got together. And threw around some more ideas, none of which I remember. But finally, Rob said he had an idea—he wanted to make a movie about a man and a woman who become friends, as opposed to lovers; they make a deliberate decision not to have sex because sex ruins everything; and then they have sex and it ruins everything. And I said, let's do it.

So we made a deal, and in February, Andy and Rob came back to New York and we sat around for several days and they told me some things. Appalling things. They told me, for instance, that when they finished having sex, they wanted to get up out of bed and go home. (Which became: HARRY: "How long do I have to lie here and hold her before I can get up and go home? Is thirty seconds enough? . . . How long do you like to be held afterwards? All night, right? . . . Somewhere between thirty seconds and all night is your problem." SALLY: "I don't have a problem.") They told me about the endless series of excuses they had concocted in order to make a middle-of-the-night getaway. (SALLY: "You know, I am so glad I never got involved with you. I just would have ended up being some woman you had to get up out of bed and leave at three o'clock in the morning and go clean your andirons. And you don't even have a fireplace. Not that I would know this.") They also told me that the reason they thought men and women couldn't be friends was that a man always wanted to sleep with a woman. Any woman. (HARRY: "No man can be friends with a woman he finds attractive. He always wants to have sex with her." SALLY: "So you're saying a man *can* be friends with a woman he finds unattractive." HARRY: "No. You pretty much want to nail them, too.") I say that these things were appalling, but the truth is that they weren't really a surprise;

they were sort of my wildest nightmares of what men thought.

Rob and Andy and I noodled for hours over the questions raised by friendship, and sex, and life in general; and as we did, I realized—long before I had any idea of what was actually going to happen in the movie itself—that I had found a wonderful character in Rob Reiner. Rob is a very strange person. He is extremely funny, but he is also extremely depressed—or at least he was at the time; he talked constantly about how depressed he was. "You know how women have a base of makeup," he said to me. "I have a base of depression. Sometimes I sink below it. Sometimes I rise above it." This line went right into the first draft of the movie, but somewhere along the line Rob cut it. A mistake, I think, but never mind. Here's another from Rob on his depression: "I think I'm not ready for a relationship. When you're as depressed as I am . . . If the depression was lifted, I would be able to be with someone on my level. But it's like playing tennis on a windy day with someone who's worse than you are. They can do all right against you, they can win a couple of games, but there's too much wind. You know what I mean?" I have no idea what Rob was talking about, but as I wrote those words in my notebook I knew that I would use the lines somehow. And I did, and they were cut, and it was a mistake, and never mind.

The point is that Rob was depressed; but he wasn't at all depressed about being depressed; in fact, he loved his depression. And so does Harry. Harry honestly believes that he is a better person than Sally because he has what Sally generously calls a dark side. "Suppose nothing happens to you," he says in the first sequence of the movie. "Suppose you live there [New York] your whole life and nothing happens. You never meet anyone, you never become anything, and finally you die one of those New York deaths where nobody notices for two weeks until the smell drifts out into the hallway." Harry is genuinely proud to have thought of that possibility and to lay it at the feet of this shallow young woman he is stuck in a car with for eighteen hours. He is thrilled to be the prince of darkness, the master of the worst-case scenario, the man who is happy to tell you, as you find yourself in the beginning of a love affair, that what follows lust, inevitably, is post-lust: "You take someone to the airport, it's clearly the beginning of a relationship. That's why I've never taken anyone to the airport at the beginning of a relationship. . . . Because eventually things move on and you don't take someone to the airport, and I never wanted anyone to say to me, 'How come you never take me to the airport anymore?' "

So I began with a Harry, based on Rob. And because Harry was bleak and depressed, it followed absolutely that Sally would be cheerful and chirpy and relentlessly, pointlessly, unrealistically, idiotically optimistic. Which is, it turns out, very much like me. I'm not precisely chirpy, but I am the sort of person who is fine, I'm just fine, everything's fine. "I am over him," Sally says, when she isn't over him at all; I have uttered that line far too many times in my life, and far too many times I've made the mistake of believing it was true. Sally loves control—and I'm sorry to say that I do too. And inevitably, Sally's need to control her environment is connected to food. I say inevitably because food has always been something I write about—in part because it's the only thing I'm an expert on. But it wasn't my idea to use the way I order food as a character trait for Sally; well along in the process—third or fourth draft or so—Rob and Andy and I were ordering lunch for the fifth day in a row, and for the fifth day in a row my lunch order—for an avocado and bacon sandwich—consisted of an endless series of paren-

thetical remarks. I wanted the mayonnaise on the side. I
wanted the bread toasted and slightly burnt. I wanted the
bacon crisp. "I just like it the way I like it," I said, defensively, when the pattern was pointed out to me—and the
line went into the script.

But all that came much later. In the beginning, I was
more or less alone—with a male character based somewhat
on Rob, and a female character based somewhat on me. And
a subject. Which was not, by the way, whether men and
women could be friends. The movie instead was a way for
me to write about being single—about the difficult, frustrat-
ing, awful, funny search for happiness in an American city
where the primary emotion is unrequited love. This is from
my notes, February 5, 1985, Rob speaking: "This is a talk
piece. There are no chase scenes. No food fights. This is
walks, apartments, phones, restaurants, movies." Also from
my notes, Rob again: "We're talking about a movie about
two people who get each other from the breakup of the first
big relationship in their lives to the beginning of the second.
Transitional on some level. Who are friends, who don't have
sex, who nurse each other and comfort each other and talk
to each other and then finally do it and it's a mistake and
recover from it and move into second relationships." Here's
a scene from the first draft; it bit the dust early, too self-
conscious, but I toss it in partly because I can't stand to
waste anything, and partly because it perfectly sums up the
movie I was trying to write:

SALLY   I think we should write a movie about our
relationship.

HARRY   What's the plot?

SALLY   There are only two plots. The first is, an
appealing character strives against great odds to

achieve a worthwhile goal, and the second is, the bluebird of happiness is right in your own backyard. We're the first.

HARRY   An appealing character—

SALLY   *Two* appealing characters strive against great odds to achieve a worthwhile goal. Two people become friends at the end of the first major relationship of their lives and get each other to the next major relationship of their lives.

HARRY   I don't know anything about writing movies.

SALLY   Neither do I.

HARRY   But on the face of it—I don't want to be negative about it—

SALLY   Sure you do. You love being negative, it's who you are, embrace it—

HARRY   —but it seems to me that movies are supposed to be visual. We don't do anything visual. We just sit in restaurants and talk, or we sit on the phone and talk, or we sit in your apartment or my apartment and talk.

SALLY   In French movies they just talk.

HARRY   Do you speak French?

SALLY   Not really.

HARRY   What happens to the friends when each of them gets to the next major relationship of their lives?

SALLY   They're still going to be friends. They're going to be friends forever.

HARRY   I don't know, Sally. You know what happens. You meet somebody new and you take them to meet your friend, and you want them to like each other as much as you do, but they never do, they always see the friend as a threat to your relationship, and you try to stay just as good friends with your friend but eventually you don't really need each other as much because you've got a new friend, you've got someone you can talk to *and* fuck—

SALLY   Forget I mentioned it, okay?

They smile at each other.

HARRY   I love you. You know that.

SALLY   I love you too.

HARRY   When I say, "I love you," you know what I mean—

SALLY   I know what you mean. I know.

When Harry Met Sally started shooting in August 1988, almost four years after my first meeting with Rob and Andy. In the meantime I wrote a first draft about two people who get each other from the breakup of the first big relationship in their lives to the beginning of the second. Rob went off and made *Stand By Me*. We met again and decided that Harry and Sally belonged together. I wrote a second draft. Rob went off and made *The Princess Bride*. And then we all went to work together on the next (at least) five drafts of the movie. What had been called *Just Friends* and then *Play Melancholy Baby* went on to be called *Boy Meets Girl; Words of Love; It Had to Be You;* and *Harry, This Is Sally*. To name just a few of the titles. Mostly we called it "Untitled Rob Reiner Project." Rob suggested that we try inserting some older couples talking about how they met. *How They Met* was another title we considered for at least a day. And gradually, the script began to change, from something that was mostly mine, to something else.

Here is what I always say about screenwriting. When you write a script, it's like delivering a great big beautiful plain pizza, the one with only cheese and tomatoes. And then you give it to the director, and the director says, "I love this pizza. I am willing to commit to this pizza. But I really think this pizza should have mushrooms on it." And you say, "Mushrooms! Of course! I meant to put mushrooms on the pizza! Why didn't I think of that? Let's put some on immediately." And then someone else comes along and says, "I love this pizza too, but it really needs green peppers." "Great," you say. "Green peppers. Just the thing." And then someone else says, "Anchovies." There's always a fight over the anchovies. And when you get done, what you have is a pizza with everything. Sometimes it's wonderful. And sometimes you look at it and you think, I knew we shouldn't have put the green peppers onto it. Why didn't I say so at the time? Why didn't I lie down in traffic to prevent anyone's putting green peppers onto the pizza?

All this is a long way of saying that movies generally start out belonging to the writer and end up belonging to the director. If you're very lucky as a writer, you look at the director's movie and feel that it's your movie, too. As Rob and Andy and I worked on the movie, it changed: it became less quirky and much funnier; it became less mine and more theirs. But what made it possible for me to live through this process—which is actually called "The Process," a polite expression for the period when the writer, generally, gets screwed—was that Rob and I each had a character we owned. On most movies, what normally happens in the course of The Process is that the writer says one thing and the director says another thing, and in the end the most the writer can hope for is a compromise; what made this movie different was that Rob had a character who could say whatever he believed, and if I disagreed, I had Sally to say so for me.

And much as I would like to take full credit for what

Sally says in the movie, the fact is that many of her best moments went into the script after the three of us began work on it together. "We told you about men," Rob and Andy said to me one day. "Now tell us about women." So I said, "Well, we could do something about sex fantasies." And I wrote the scene about Sally's sex fantasy. "What else?" they said. "Well," I said, "women send flowers to themselves in order to fool their boyfriends into thinking they have other suitors." And I wrote the scene about Marie sending flowers to herself. "What else?" Rob and Andy said. "Well," I said, "women fake orgasms." "Really?" they said. "Yes," I said. There was a long pause. I think I am correct in remembering the long pause. "All women?" they said. "Most women," I said. "At one time or another."

A few days later, Rob called. He and Andy had written a sequence about faking orgasms and they wanted to insert it at the end of the scene that was known (up to that time) as the andirons scene. He read it over the phone. I loved it. It went into the script. A few weeks later, we had our first actors' reading, and Meg Ryan, who by then was our Sally, suggested that Sally actually fake an orgasm in the delicatessen at the end of the scene. We loved it. It went into the script. And then Billy Crystal, our Harry, provided the funniest of the dozens of funny lines he brought with him to the movie; he suggested that a woman customer turn to a waiter, when Sally's orgasm was over, and say: "I'll have what she's having." The line, by the way, was delivered in the movie by Estelle Reiner, Rob's mother. So there you have it—a perfect example of how The Process works on the occasions when it works.

I don't want to sound Pollyannaish about any of this. Rob and I disagreed. We disagreed all the time. Rob believes that men and women can't be friends (HARRY: "Men and women can't be friends, because the sex part always gets in the way"). I disagree (SALLY: "That's not true. I have plenty of men friends and there's no sex involved"). And both of us are right. Which brings me to what *When Harry Met Sally* is really about—not, as I said, whether men and women can be friends, but about how different men and women are. The truth is that men don't want to be friends with women. Men know they don't understand women, and they don't much care. They want women as lovers, as wives, as mothers, but they're not really interested in them as friends. They have friends. Men are their friends. And they talk to their male friends about sports, and I have no idea what else.

Women, on the other hand, are dying to be friends with men. Women know they don't understand men, and it bothers them: they think that if only they could be friends with them, they would understand them and, what's more (and this is their gravest mistake), it would help. Women think if they could just understand men, they could *do something.* Women are always trying to *do something.* There are entire industries based on this premise, the most obvious one being the women's magazines—there are hundreds of them, there are probably five of them in darkest Zaire alone—that are based completely on the notion that women can *do something* where men are concerned: cook a perfect steak, or wear a perfect skirt, or dab a little perfume behind the knee. "Rub your thighs together when you walk," someone once wrote in *Cosmopolitan* magazine. "The squish-squish sound of nylon has a frenzying effect."

When a movie like *When Harry Met Sally* opens, people come to ask you questions about it. And for a few brief weeks, you become an expert. You seem quite wise. You give the impression that you knew what you were doing all along. You become an expert on friends, on the possibilities of love, on the differences between men and women. But the truth is that when you work on a movie, you don't sit around thinking, We're making a movie about the difference between men and women. Or whatever. You just do it. You say, this scene works for me, but this one doesn't. You say, this is good, but this could be funnier. You say, it's a little slow here, what could we do to speed it up? You say, this scene is long, and this scene isn't story, and we need a better button on this one.

And then they go off and shoot the movie and cut the movie and sometimes you get a movie that you're happy with. It's my experience that this happens very rarely. Once in a blue moon. *Blue Moon* was another title we considered for a minute or two. I mention it now so you will understand that even when you have a movie you're happy with, there's always something—in this case, the title—that you wish you could fix. But never mind.

When Harry Met Sally...

FADE IN:

DOCUMENTARY FOOTAGE

of an OLDER COUPLE, a MAN and a WOMAN. They're sitting together on a love seat looking straight at the CAMERA.

MAN   I was sitting with my friend Arthur Kornblum, in a restaurant, it was a Horn and Hardart Cafeteria, and this beautiful girl walked in—   *(he points to the woman beside him)*   —and I turned to Arthur and I said, "Arthur, you see that girl? I'm going to marry her." And two weeks later we were married. And it's over fifty years later and we're still married.

FADE OUT.

FADE IN:

EXT. UNIVERSITY OF CHICAGO CAMPUS—DAY

CARD: UNIVERSITY OF CHICAGO—1977
A couple in a clinch.

The young man involved is named HARRY BURNS. He's twenty-six years old, just graduated from law school. Wearing jeans and a sweat-shirt.

He's kissing a young woman named AMANDA. She has long, straight hair that she irons. She's about twenty. The embrace is fairly melodramatic. They pull back to look at one another.

AMANDA   I love you.

HARRY   I love you.

They begin to kiss again.

A car pulls up right beside them. Stops. Sits there.

Driving the car is SALLY ALBRIGHT. She's twenty-one years old. She's very pretty although not necessarily in an obvious way. She sits there waiting for the kiss to end. It doesn't end. She clears her throat.

Amanda sees Sally, and she and Harry move over to the car.

AMANDA   Oh. Hi, Sally. Sally, this is Harry Burns. Harry, this is Sally Albright.

HARRY   Nice to meet you.

They shake hands.

SALLY   *(to Harry)*   You want to drive the first shift?

HARRY   No, no, you're there already, you can start.

SALLY   Back's open.

Harry looks meaningfully at Amanda.

Then he starts to put his stuff—a duffel bag, a box of records—into the back seat of the car, where Sally's stuff is, too—suitcases, stereo speakers, a guitar, boxes of books, a small TV.

AMANDA   Call me.

HARRY   I'll call as soon as I get there.

AMANDA   Call me from the road.

HARRY   I'll call before that.

Harry and Amanda exchange longing looks outside the car.

AMANDA   I love you.

HARRY I love you.

They kiss again.

Sally sits waiting, waiting. She shifts position and accidentally-on-purpose hits the car HORN, which beeps and startles Amanda and Harry into breaking off their clinch.

SALLY Sorry.

HARRY I miss you already.

AMANDA I miss you.

HARRY Bye.

Harry gets into the car, and Amanda watches it pull away.

CUT TO:

INT. CAR—DAY
Harry takes out a bunch of grapes, starts to eat them.

SALLY I have it all figured out. It's an eighteen-hour trip, which breaks down to six shifts of three hours each. Or, alternatively, we could break it down by mileage. There's a map on the visor that I've marked to show the locations where we change shifts.

HARRY *(offering her one)* Grape?

SALLY No. I don't like to eat between meals.

Harry spits a grape seed out the window, which doesn't happen to be down.

HARRY I'll roll down the window.

After a lengthy silence.

HARRY (CONT'D) Why don't you tell me the story of your life?

SALLY The story of my life?

HARRY We've got eighteen hours to kill before we hit New York.

SALLY   The story of my life isn't even going to get us out of Chicago. I mean, nothing's happened to me yet. That's why I'm going to New York.

HARRY   So something can happen to you?

SALLY   Yes.

HARRY   Like what?

SALLY   Like I'm going to go to journalism school to become a reporter.

HARRY   So you can write about things that happen to other people.

SALLY   *(after a beat)*   That's one way to look at it.

HARRY   Suppose nothing happens to you. Suppose you live there your whole life and nothing happens. You never meet anyone, you never become anything, and finally you die one of those New York deaths where nobody notices for two weeks until the smell drifts out into the hallway.

Sally looks over at Harry. Who am I stuck in this car with? She looks back at the road.

EXT. CAR—TRAVELING SHOT—DAY
As the car turns onto the highway.

SALLY   *(Voice-over)*   Amanda mentioned you had a dark side.

HARRY   That's what drew her to me.

SALLY   Your dark side?

HARRY   Sure. Why? Don't you have a dark side? I know, you're probably one of those cheerful people who dot their "i's" with little hearts.

SALLY   *(defensively)*   I have just as much of a dark side as the next person—

HARRY *(pleased with himself)* Oh, really? When I buy a new book, I read the last page first. That way, in case I die before I finish, I know how it ends. That, my friend, is a dark side.

SALLY *(irritated now)* That doesn't mean you're deep or anything. I mean, yes, basically I'm a happy person . . .

HARRY *(cheerfully)* So am I.

SALLY . . . and I don't see that there's anything wrong with that.

HARRY Of course not. You're too busy being happy. Do you ever think about death?

SALLY Yes.

HARRY Sure you do. A fleeting thought that drifts in and out of the transom of your mind. I spend hours, I spend days—

SALLY *(interrupting)* —and you think this makes you a better person?

HARRY Look, when the shit comes down, I'm going to be prepared and you're not, that's all I'm saying.

SALLY And in the meantime, you're going to ruin your whole life waiting for it.

DISSOLVE TO:

EXT. CAR—DAY
The car tooling along a beautiful stretch of highway.

SALLY *(Voice-over)* You're wrong.

HARRY *(Voice-over)* I'm not wrong.

SALLY *(Voice-over)* You're wrong.

HARRY *(Voice-over)* He wants her to leave. That's why he puts her on the plane.

SALLY *(Voice-over)* I don't think *she* wants to stay.

HARRY *(Voice-over)* Of course she wants to stay. Wouldn't you rather be with Humphrey Bogart than that other guy?

EXT.—CAR EXITING (INDUSTRIAL)—MAGIC HOUR

EXT.—DINER—NIGHT
Sally's car rounds the corner near some refinery tanks, heads into a diner parking lot.

SALLY *(Voice-over)* I don't want to spend the rest of my life in Casablanca married to a man who runs a bar. That probably sounds very snobbish to you, but I don't.

The car pulls up in front of a diner straight out of the fifties, Harry driving.

HARRY *(Voice-over)* You'd rather have a passionless marriage—

SALLY *(Voice-over)* —and be First Lady of Czechoslovakia—

HARRY *(Voice-over)* —than live with the man . . .

INT. CAR—NIGHT

HARRY . . . you've had the greatest sex of your life with, just because he owns a bar and that's all he does.

SALLY Yes, and so would any woman in her right mind. Women are very practical.

Sally takes out a can of hairspray, sprays her hair.

SALLY (CONT'D) Even Ingrid Bergman, which is why she gets on that plane at the end of the movie.

EXT. DINER PARKING LOT—NIGHT

HARRY *(getting out of car)* Oh, I understand.

SALLY *(getting out of car)* What? What?

HARRY Nothing.

Harry crosses toward the diner. Sally follows after him.

SALLY What?

HARRY Forget about it.

SALLY What? What? Forget about what?

He doesn't answer and heads up the stairs to the diner, Sally following.

SALLY (CONT'D) Now just tell me.

HARRY Obviously you haven't had great sex.

He goes inside the diner. She follows.

INT. DINER—NIGHT

HARRY *(to the hostess)* Table for two.

SALLY Yes, I have.

HARRY No, you haven't.

He crosses away from her toward the table.

SALLY It just so happens I have had plenty of good sex.

This doesn't go unheard by the hostess and other diners. Sally walks to the table, sits down.

HARRY With whom?

SALLY What?

HARRY With whom have you had this great sex?

SALLY *(embarrassed)* I'm not going to tell you that.

HARRY Fine. Don't tell me.

A long silence. Harry looks at the menu. Sally opens hers but doesn't read it.

SALLY Shel Gordon.

HARRY Shel. Sheldon? No. You did not have great sex with Sheldon.

SALLY   I did too.

HARRY   No, you didn't. A Sheldon can do your taxes. If you need a root canal, Sheldon is your man, but humping and pumping is not Sheldon's strong suit. It's the name. "Do it to me, Sheldon." "You're an animal, Sheldon." "Ride me, big Sheldon." It doesn't work.

A WAITRESS approaches the table.

WAITRESS   What can I get you?

HARRY   I'll have the Number Three.

The Waitress turns to Sally.

SALLY   I'd like the chef salad, please, with the oil and vinegar on the side. And the apple pie à la mode.

WAITRESS   *(writing)*   Chef and apple à la mode.

SALLY   But I'd like the pie heated, and I don't want the ice cream on top, I want it on the side. And I'd like strawberry instead of vanilla if you have it. If not, then no ice cream, just whipped cream, but only if it's real. If it's out of a can, then nothing.

WAITRESS   Not even the pie?

SALLY   No, just the pie. But then not heated.

As the Waitress leaves, Harry stares in disbelief at Sally.

SALLY (CONT'D)   What?

HARRY   Nothing. Nothing. So how come you broke up with Sheldon?

SALLY   How do you know we broke up?

HARRY   Because if you didn't break up, you wouldn't be with me, you'd be off with Sheldon the Wonder Schlong.

SALLY   First of all, I'm not *with* you. And second of all, it's none of your business why we broke up.

HARRY   You're right, you're right. I don't want to know.

After a beat:

SALLY   Well, if you must know, it was because he was very jealous and I had these Days of the Week underpants.

HARRY   *(makes a buzzer sound)*   I'm sorry, I need a judge's ruling on this. Days of the Week underpants?

SALLY   Yes. They had the days of the week on them, I thought they were sort of funny—and one day Sheldon says to me, "You never wear Sunday." He's all suspicious. Where was Sunday? Where had I left Sunday? And I told him, and he didn't believe me.

HARRY   What?

SALLY   They don't make Sunday.

HARRY   Why not?

SALLY   Because of God.

DISSOLVE TO:

EXT. DINER—NIGHT—REESTABLISH

INT. DINER—NIGHT

They are finishing their meal. Sally figures out her portion of the bill.

SALLY   Fifteen percent of my share is . . .
(writes)   Six-ninety . . . leave seven. . . .

She notices Harry just staring at her.

SALLY (CONT'D)   *(thinking she might have some food on her face, she nervously wipes)*   What? Do I have something on my face?

HARRY   You're a very attractive person.

SALLY   Thank you.

HARRY   Amanda never said how attractive you were.

SALLY   Well, maybe she doesn't think I'm attractive.

HARRY   I don't think it's a matter of opinion. Empirically, you are attractive.

They get up to leave.

SALLY   Amanda is my friend.

Harry throws down a crumpled bill, and they head for the door.

HARRY   So?

SALLY   So you're going with her.

HARRY   So?

SALLY   So you're coming on to me.

EXT. DINER—NIGHT

HARRY   *(coming out of door)*   No, I wasn't.

Sally looks at him.

HARRY (CONT'D)   What? Can't a man say a woman is attractive without it being a come-on?

Harry walks to the driver's side as Sally is unlocking the passenger door.

HARRY (CONT'D)   All right, all right.

Both walk into the foreground, meeting. Sally moves away from him, upset.

HARRY (CONT'D)   Let's just say, just for the sake of argument, that it was a come-on. Okay. What do you want me to do about it? I take it back, okay? I take it back.

SALLY   You can't take it back.

HARRY   Why not?

SALLY   Because it's already out there.

An awkward pause.

HARRY   Oh, jeez. What are we supposed to do? Call the cops? It's already out there!

SALLY   Just let it lie, okay?

HARRY   Great! Let it lie. That's my policy. That's what I always say.

They both get in the car.

INT. CAR—NIGHT

HARRY   Let it lie.   *(beat)*   Want to spend the night in a motel?

Sally glares at him.

HARRY (CONT'D)   See what I did? I didn't let it lie.

SALLY   Harry—

HARRY   I said I would and then I didn't—

SALLY   Harry—

HARRY   I went the other way—

SALLY   Harry—

HARRY   What?

SALLY   We are just going to be friends, okay?

HARRY   Great. Friends. The best thing.

As the car starts up and pulls out, we—

CUT TO:

EXT. HIGHWAY—NIGHT
As the car tools along, we hear

HARRY   *(Voice-over)*   You realize, of course, that we could never be friends.

SALLY   *(Voice-over)*   Why not?

INT. CAR—NIGHT
Sally is driving.

HARRY What I'm saying—and this is not a come-on in any way, shape, or form—is that men and women can't be friends, because the sex part always gets in the way.

SALLY That's not true. I have a number of men friends and there's no sex involved.

HARRY No, you don't.

SALLY Yes, I do.

HARRY No, you don't.

SALLY Yes, I do.

HARRY You only think you do.

SALLY You're saying I'm having sex with these men without my knowledge?

HARRY No, I'm saying they all *want* to have sex with you.

SALLY They do not.

HARRY Do too.

SALLY They do not.

HARRY Do too.

SALLY How do you know?

HARRY Because no man can be friends with a woman he finds attractive. He always wants to have sex with her.

SALLY So you're saying a man *can* be friends with a woman he finds unattractive.

HARRY No. You pretty much want to nail them, too.

SALLY What if *they* don't want to have sex with *you?*

HARRY Doesn't matter, because the sex thing is

already out there, so the friendship is ultimately doomed, and that is the end of the story.

SALLY   Well, I guess we're not going to be friends, then.

HARRY   Guess not.

SALLY   That's too bad.   *(beat)*   You were the only person I knew in New York.

DISSOLVE TO:

EXT. NEW YORK SKYLINE—DAWN
As the car comes over the George Washington Bridge. A gorgeous day.

DISSOLVE TO:

EXT. NEW YORK STREET CORNER—DAY
Downtown near Washington Square. The car pulls up and Harry hops out, grabbing his stuff. Sally also walks to the back of the car.

HARRY   Thanks for the ride.

SALLY   Yeah. It was interesting.

HARRY   It was nice knowing you.

SALLY   Yeah.

Sally nods. Harry nods. An awkward moment.

Sally holds out her hand. They shake.

SALLY (CONT'D)   Well, have a nice life.

HARRY   You too.

Harry starts to walk off.

As she drives off.

FADE OUT.

FADE IN:

DOCUMENTARY FOOTAGE
Another OLDER COUPLE sitting together on the same love seat we saw earlier.

SECOND WOMAN   We fell in love in high school—

SECOND MAN   Yeah, we were high school sweethearts.

SECOND WOMAN   But then after our junior year, his parents moved away.

SECOND MAN   I never forgot her.

SECOND WOMAN   He never forgot me.

SECOND MAN   Her face was burned on my brain. And it was thirty-four years later that I was walking down Broadway and I see her coming out of Toffenetti's.

SECOND WOMAN   And we both looked at each other, and it was just as though not a single day had gone by.

SECOND MAN   She was just as beautiful as she was at sixteen.

SECOND WOMAN   He was just the same. He looked exactly the same.

FADE OUT.

FADE IN:

INT. LA GUARDIA AIRPORT—DAY

IT'S FIVE YEARS LATER.

A couple in a clinch.

The woman is Sally at twenty-six. She looks great, she's a stylish young woman.

She's kissing a very attractive man, although it's not that easy to see him at the moment. His name is JOE.

Harry is coming down the hallway of the airline terminal. He's wearing a suit and tie and trench coat; he has a kind of attractive-but-rumpled demeanor. He notices the couple kissing. Goes past them. Then stops. Backs up. He recognizes them.

They're still kissing.

Harry comes closer, peers at the two of them from slightly too close. It's not easy to see either of their faces.

Finally, Sally and Joe become aware that someone is standing nearby, and they stop kissing to look at Harry.

HARRY   Joe—I thought it was you. I thought it was you! *(shaking hands)*   Harry Burns.

JOE   Harry, Harry, how ya doing?

HARRY   Good. How you doing?

JOE   I'm just fine. I'm doing fine.

HARRY   I was just walking by, and I thought it was you, and here it is, it's you.

JOE   Yeah, yeah, it was.

HARRY   You still with the D.A.'s Office?

JOE   No, I switched to the other side.

HARRY   Oh.

JOE   What about you?

HARRY   I'm working with this small company, doing political consulting.

JOE   Oh yeah?

HARRY   Yeah, it's been great. Yeah.

Joe nods. Harry nods. An awkward pause. Sally just standing there, wondering if Harry remembers her.

JOE   Oh Harry, this is Sally Albright. Harry Burns.

Harry nods and smiles.

JOE (CONT'D)   Harry and I used to live in the same building.

Sally nods. Harry knows he's seen her someplace but he can't remember where.

HARRY Well, listen, I got a plane to catch. It was really good to see you, Joe.

JOE You too, Harry.

HARRY *(to Sally)* Bye.

Harry starts down the long corridor for his plane. Joe and Sally look at each other.

SALLY Thank God he couldn't place me. I drove from college to New York with him five years ago and it was the longest night of my life.

JOE What happened?

SALLY He made a pass at me, and when I said no—he was going with a girlfriend of mine—oh God, I can't remember her name. Don't get involved with me, Joe, I'm twenty-six years old and I can't even remember the name of the girl I was such good friends with that I wouldn't get involved with her boyfriend.

JOE So what happened?

SALLY When?

JOE When he made a pass at you and you said no.

SALLY Uh . . . I said we could just be friends, and—this part I remember—he said men and women could never really be friends.

Joe smiles, shakes his head.

SALLY (CONT'D) Do you think that's true?

JOE No.

SALLY Do you have any women friends? Just friends?

JOE No, but I'll get one if it's important to you.

Sally smiles, then she and Joe move close to kiss. Suddenly Sally pulls back.

SALLY Amanda Reese. Thank God.

JOE I'm going to miss you. *(beat)* I love you.

SALLY *(it's the first time he's said it)* You do?

JOE Yes.

SALLY I love you.

They kiss.

CUT TO:

INT. AIRPLANE—DAY

The plane is in flight, en route from New York to Washington.

Sally is in a middle seat in a crowded all-coach plane. She has The New York Times *on her lap, but she's staring into the middle distance, a little smile on her face.*

There's a MAN ON THE AISLE next to her.

In the row in back of her, in the aisle seat, is Harry. His head pops up.

Sally starts to read the newspaper. The Man on the Aisle looks up at Harry, who's still looming over him, trying to place Sally. Harry pops down.

The STEWARDESS comes down the aisle with the drink cart.

STEWARDESS And what would you like to drink?

SALLY Do you have any Bloody Mary mix?

STEWARDESS Yes.

She starts to pour.

SALLY No, wait. Here's what I want. Regular tomato juice, filled about three quarters, and add a splash of Bloody Mary mix, just a splash, and . . .

Harry's head starts to rise again.

SALLY (CONT'D) . . . a little piece of lime, but on the side.

HARRY The University of Chicago, right?

Sally turns, sees Harry, then turns back around.

SALLY   Yes.

HARRY   Did you look this good at the University of Chicago?

SALLY   No.

HARRY   *(he's being mischievous here)*   Did we ever—?

SALLY   *(laughing; she can't believe him)*   No. No!   *(to Man on the Aisle)*   We drove from Chicago to New York together after graduation.

The Man on the Aisle has been listening and watching all this.

MAN ON THE AISLE   *(to Harry)*   Would you two like to sit together?

SALLY   No.

HARRY   Great! Thank you.

Harry and the Man on the Aisle change seats and Harry sits down next to Sally.

HARRY (CONT'D)   You were a friend of . . . um . . .

He can't remember her name.

SALLY   Amanda's. I can't believe you can't remember her name.

HARRY   What do you mean? I can remember. Amanda. Right? Amanda Rice.

SALLY   Reese.

HARRY   Reese, right. That's what I said. Whatever happened to her?

SALLY   I have no idea.

HARRY   You have no idea? You were really good friends with her. We didn't make it because you were such good friends.

SALLY   You went with her.

HARRY   And was it worth it? This sacrifice for a friend you haven't even kept in touch with?

SALLY   Harry, you might not believe this, but I never considered not sleeping with you a sacrifice.

HARRY   Fair enough, fair enough.

After a beat:

HARRY (CONT'D)   You were going to be a gymnast.

SALLY   A journalist.

HARRY   Right, that's what I said. And?

SALLY   I'm a journalist. I work at the *News.*

HARRY   Great. And you're with Joe.

Sally nods.

HARRY (CONT'D)   Well, that's great. Great. You're together—what—three weeks?

SALLY   A month. How did you know that?

HARRY   You take someone to the airport, it's clearly the beginning of a relationship. That's why I've never taken anyone to the airport at the beginning of a relationship.

SALLY   Why?

HARRY   Because eventually things move on and you don't take someone to the airport, and I never wanted anyone to say to me, "How come you never take me to the airport anymore?"

SALLY   It's amazing. You look like a normal person, but actually you're the Angel of Death.

HARRY   Are you going to marry him?

SALLY   We've only known each other a month, and

besides, neither one of us is looking to get married right now.

HARRY   I'm getting married.

SALLY   You are?

HARRY   *(matter-of-factly)*   Um-hmm.

SALLY   *You* are?

HARRY   Yeah.

SALLY   Who is she?

HARRY   Helen Hillson. She's a lawyer. She's keeping her name.

SALLY   *(shakes her head)*   You're getting married.

She laughs.

HARRY   Yeah. What's so funny about it?

SALLY   It's just so optimistic of you, Harry.

HARRY   Well, you'd be amazed what falling madly in love can do for you.

SALLY   Well, it's wonderful. It's nice to see you embracing life in this manner.

HARRY   Yeah, plus, you know, you just get to a certain point where you get tired of the whole thing.

SALLY   What whole thing?

HARRY   The whole life-of-a-single-guy thing. You meet someone, you have the safe lunch, you decide you like each other enough to move on to dinner, you go dancing, you do the white man's overbite, you go back to her place, you have sex, and the minute you're finished, you know what goes through your mind? *(Sally shakes her head no)*   How long do I have to lie here and hold her before I can get up and go home? Is thirty seconds enough?

SALLY   That's what you're thinking? Is that true?

HARRY   Sure. All men think that. How long do you like to be held afterwards? All night, right? See, that's the problem. Somewhere between thirty seconds and all night is your problem.

SALLY   I don't have a problem.

HARRY   Yeah you do.

                                                    CUT TO:

EXT. NATIONAL AIRPORT—DAY
As the plane lands.

INT. NATIONAL AIRPORT—DAY
Harry and Sally are on a moving sidewalk, Harry several steps behind Sally. He makes his way past the other passengers to stand by her.

HARRY   Staying over?

SALLY   Yes.

HARRY   Would you like to have dinner?

Sally looks at him suspiciously.

HARRY (CONT'D)   Just friends.

SALLY   I thought you didn't believe men and women could be friends.

HARRY   When did I say that?

SALLY   On the ride to New York.

HARRY   No, no, no, no. I never said that. *(reconsiders)* Yes, that's right. They can't be friends . . . *(figuring this out)* . . . unless both of them are involved with other people. Then they can. This is an amendment to the earlier rule. If the two people are in relationships, the pressure of possible involvement is lifted.
(thinking this over)   That doesn't work either. Because what happens then, the person you're involved with

doesn't understand why you need to be friends with the person you're just friends with, like it means something is missing from the relationship and you have to go outside to get it. Then when you say, "No, no, no, it's not true, nothing is missing from the relationship," the person you're involved with then accuses you of being secretly attracted to the person you're just friends with, which you probably are—I mean, come on, who the hell are we kidding, let's face it—which brings us back to the earlier rule before the amendment, that men and women can't be friends. So where does that leave us?

SALLY   Harry—

HARRY   What?

SALLY   Goodbye.

HARRY   Okay.

> *They look at each other. Though they have said goodbye, they are now in that awkward place of still going in the same direction next to each other on the moving sidewalk. After a beat:*

HARRY (CONT'D)   I'll just stop walking, I'll let you go ahead.

FADE OUT.

FADE IN:

> DOCUMENTARY FOOTAGE
> *Another OLDER COUPLE sitting on a love seat, looking at the CAMERA.*

THIRD MAN   We were married forty years ago. We were married three years. We got a divorce. Then I married Marjorie.

THIRD WOMAN   But first you lived with Barbara.

THIRD MAN   Right. Barbara. But I didn't marry Barbara. I married Marjorie.

THIRD WOMAN   Then you got a divorce.

THIRD MAN   Right. Then I married Katie.

THIRD WOMAN   Another divorce.

THIRD MAN   Then, a couple of years later at Eddie Callichio's funeral, I ran into her. I was with some girl I don't even remember.

THIRD WOMAN   Roberta.

THIRD MAN   Right, Roberta. But I couldn't take my eyes off you. *(beat)*   I remember, I snuck over to her and I said—what did I say?

THIRD WOMAN   You said, "What are you doing after?"

THIRD MAN   Right. So I ditched Roberta, we go for coffee, a month later we're married.

THIRD WOMAN   Thirty-five years to the day after our first marriage.

FADE OUT.

EXT. NEW YORK RESTAURANT WITH VIEW—DAY

IT'S FIVE YEARS LATER.
Sally is sitting at a table with two other women, MARIE and ALICE. Marie is a dark-haired, dark-eyed beauty. Alice is cute and plump, a married lady.

MARIE   So, I go through his pockets, okay?

ALICE   Marie, why do you go through his pockets?

MARIE   You know what I found?

ALICE   No, what?

MARIE   They just bought a dining-room table. He and

his wife just went out and spent $1,600 on a dining-room table.

ALICE Where?

MARIE The point isn't where, Alice. The point is, he's never going to leave her.

ALICE So what else is new? You've known this for two years.

MARIE *(glumly)* You're right, you're right. I know you're right.

ALICE Why can't you find someone single? When I was single, I knew lots of nice, single men. There must be someone. Sally found someone.

MARIE Sally got the last good one.

SALLY *(matter-of-factly)* Joe and I broke up.

ALICE What?

MARIE When?

SALLY Monday.

ALICE You waited three days to tell us?

MARIE You mean Joe's available?

ALICE For God's sake, Marie—don't you have any feelings about this? She's obviously upset.

SALLY I'm not that upset. We've been growing apart for quite a while.

MARIE *(horrified)* But you guys were a couple. You had someone to go places with. You had a date on national holidays.

SALLY I said to myself, you deserve more than this, you're thirty-one years old—

MARIE —and the clock is ticking.

SALLY No, the clock doesn't really start to tick until you're thirty-six.

ALICE God. You're in such great shape.

SALLY Well, I've had a few days to get used to it, and I feel okay.

MARIE Good. Then you're ready.

Marie takes her Rolodex out of her satchel and starts to look through it.

ALICE *(aghast)* Really, Marie.

MARIE Well, how else do you think you do it?

She flips through the Rolodex and pulls out a card.

MARIE (CONT'D) I've got the perfect guy. I don't happen to find him attractive, but you might. *(to Alice, indicating Sally)* She doesn't have a problem with chins.

SALLY Marie, I'm not ready yet.

MARIE But you just said you were over him.

SALLY I am over him. But I am in a mourning period. *(beat)* Who is it?

MARIE Alex Anderson.

SALLY You fixed me up with him six years ago.

MARIE Sorry . . .

SALLY God.

MARIE *(pulls another card)* All right, wait. Here—here we go. Ken Darman.

SALLY He's been married for over a year.

MARIE Really? Married.

Marie takes Ken Darman's Rolodex card and dog-ears a corner of it and places it in a section at the back of the box. Then she pulls out another card.

MARIE (CONT'D)   Oh wait, wait, wait, I got one.

SALLY   Look, there is no point in my going out with someone I might really like if I met him at the right time but who right now has no chance of being anything to me but a transitional man.

MARIE   Okay. But don't wait too long. Remember what happened to David Warsaw? His wife left him, and everyone said, give him some time, don't move in too fast. *Six months later he was dead.*

SALLY   What are you saying? I should get married to someone right away in case he's about to die?

ALICE   At least you can say you were married.

MARIE   I'm saying that the right man for you might be out there right now and if you don't grab him, someone else will, and you'll have to spend the rest of your life knowing that someone else is married to your husband.

CUT TO:

EXT. GIANTS STADIUM—DAY
A wave is in progress. It sweeps around the stadium and passes by Harry and his friend JESS, sitting in the second deck surrounded by Giants fans. It's fall, they're both wearing jeans and windbreakers.

Harry is very despondent.

JESS   When did this happen?

HARRY   Friday, Helen comes home from work, and she says, "I don't know if I want to be married anymore." Like it's the institution, you know, like it's nothing personal, just something she's been thinking about in a casual way. I'm calm. I say, "Why don't we take some time to think about it?" You know, don't rush into anything.

JESS   Yeah, right.

HARRY   Next day she says she's thought about it, and she wants a trial separation. She just wants to *try* it, she says. But we can still date, she says, like this is supposed to cushion the blow. I mean, I got married so I could stop dating, so I don't see where "we can still date" is a big incentive, since the last thing you want to do is date your wife, who's supposed to love you, which is what I'm saying to her when it occurs to me that maybe she doesn't, so I say to her, "Don't you love me anymore?" and you know what she says? "I don't know if I've ever loved you."

A wave comes through the crowd, and Harry and Jess stand and wave their hands.

JESS   Ooh, that's harsh.

They sit down.

JESS (CONT'D)   You don't bounce back from that right away.

HARRY   Thanks, Jess.

JESS   No, I'm a writer, I know dialogue, and that's particularly harsh.

HARRY   Then she tells me that someone in her office is going to South America, and she can sublet his apartment. I can't believe this. And the doorbell rings. "I can sublet his apartment." The words are still hanging in the air, you know, like in a balloon connected to her mouth.

JESS   Like in a cartoon.

HARRY   Right. So I'm going to the door, and there are

moving men there. Now I start to get suspicious. I say, "Helen, when did you call these movers?" And she doesn't say anything, so I ask the movers, "When did this woman book you for this gig?" and they're just standing there, three huge guys, one of them wearing a T-shirt that says, "Don't fuck with Mister Zero." So I said, "Helen, when did you make this arrangement?" She says, "A week ago." I said, "You've known for a week, and you didn't tell me?" And she says, "I didn't want to ruin your birthday."

A second wave comes through and Harry and Jess stand and wave their hands.

JESS   You're saying Mister Zero knew you were getting a divorce a week before you did?

HARRY   Mister Zero knew.

JESS   I can't believe this.

HARRY   I haven't told you the bad part yet.

JESS   What could be worse than Mister Zero knowing?

HARRY   It's all a lie. She's in love with somebody else, some tax attorney. She moved in with him.

JESS   How did you find out?

HARRY   I followed her. I stood outside the building.

JESS   So humiliating.

HARRY   Tell me about it.   *(beat)*   And you know, I knew. I knew the whole time that even though we were happy, it was just an illusion and one day she would kick the shit out of me.

JESS   Marriages don't break up on account of infidelity—it's just a symptom that something else is wrong.

HARRY   Really? Well, that symptom is fucking my wife.

Another wave comes through, and they stand up. They sit down.

CUT TO:

INT. SHAKESPEARE & CO. BOOKSTORE—DAY

Sally and Marie standing in the bookstore in a section called Personal Relationships. A table full of books. Marie is looking at something like Smart Women, Foolish Choices. *Sally is looking at something like* Safe Sex in Dangerous Times.

MARIE   So I just happened to see his American Express bill.

SALLY   What do you mean, you just happened to see it?

MARIE   Well, he was shaving, and there it was in his briefcase.

SALLY   What if he came out and saw you looking through his briefcase?

MARIE   You're missing the point. I'm telling you what I found.   *(beat)*   He just spent $120 on a new nightgown for his wife.   *(beat)*   I don't think he's ever going to leave her.

SALLY   No one thinks he's ever going to leave her.

MARIE   You're right, you're right. I know you're right.

Marie looks up for a moment for a new book, sees something.

MARIE (CONT'D)   Someone is staring at you in Personal Growth.

Sally glances over to the Personal Growth section. There's Harry.

SALLY   I know him. You'd like him. He's married.

MARIE   Who is he?

SALLY   Harry Burns. He's a political consultant.

MARIE   He's cute.

SALLY   You think he's cute?

MARIE   How do you know he's married?

SALLY   Because the last time I saw him, he was getting married.

MARIE   When was that?

SALLY   Six years ago.

MARIE   So he might not be married anymore.

SALLY   Also he's obnoxious.

MARIE   This is just like in the movies, remember, like *The Lady Vanishes,* where she says to him, "You are the most obnoxious man I have ever met"—

SALLY   *(correcting her)*   —"the most contemptible"—

MARIE   And then they fall madly in love.

SALLY   Also, he never remembers me.

HARRY   Sally Albright—

SALLY   Hi, Harry—

HARRY   I thought it was you.

SALLY   It is. This is Marie . . .

Marie is exiting down the stairs. She waves goodbye.

SALLY (CONT'D)   . . . *was* Marie.

Sally turns back to Harry.

HARRY   How are you?

SALLY   Fine.

HARRY   How's Joe?

SALLY   Fine. I hear he's fine.

HARRY   You're not with Joe anymore?

SALLY   We just broke up.

HARRY Oh, I'm sorry. That's too bad.

SALLY Yeah, well, you know. Yeah. *(beat)* So, what about you?

HARRY I'm fine.

SALLY How's married life?

HARRY Not so good. I'm getting a divorce.

SALLY Oh, I'm sorry. I'm really sorry.

HARRY Yeah. Well. What are you going to do? What happened with you guys?

CUT TO:

INT. RESTAURANT—DAY
Sally and Harry having a glass of wine.

SALLY When Joe and I started seeing each other, we wanted exactly the same thing. We wanted to live together, but we didn't want to get married because every time anyone we knew got married, it ruined their relationship. They practically never had sex again. It's true, it's one of the secrets no one ever tells you. I would sit around with my girlfriends who have kids—well, actually, my one girlfriend who has kids, Alice—and she would complain about how she and Gary never did it anymore. She didn't even complain about it, now that I think about it. She just said it matter-of-factly. She said they were up all night, they were both exhausted all the time, the kids just took every sexual impulse they had out of them. And Joe and I used to talk about it, and we'd say we were so lucky to have this wonderful relationship, we can have sex on the kitchen floor and not worry about the kids walking in, we can fly off to Rome on a moment's notice. And then one day I was taking Alice's little girl for the afternoon because I'd promised to take her to the circus, and we were in a cab playing "I Spy"—I spy a mailbox, I spy a lamppost—and she looked out the window and she saw this man and this woman with these two little kids, the man had one of the kids on his shoulders, and Alice's little girl said, "I spy a family," and I started to cry. You know, I just started crying. And I went home, and I said, "The thing is, Joe, we never do fly off to Rome on a moment's notice."

HARRY   And the kitchen floor?

SALLY   Not once. It's this very cold, hard Mexican ceramic tile. Anyway, we talked about it for a long time, and I said, this is what I want, and he said, well, I don't, and I said, well, I guess it's over, and he left. And the thing is, I feel really fine. I am over him. I mean, I really am over him. That was it for him, that was the most he could give, and every time I think about it, I'm more and more convinced I did the right thing.

HARRY   Boy, you sound really healthy.

SALLY   *(not totally)*   Yeah.

CUT TO:

EXT. 77TH STREET WALK—DUSK
Harry and Sally walking together. The sun is setting.

SALLY   At least I got the apartment.

HARRY   That's what everybody says to me, too. But really, what's so hard about finding an apartment? What you do is, you read the obituary column. Yeah. You find out who died, go to the building, and then you tip the doorman. What they can do to make it easier is to combine the obituaries with the real estate section, see, and then you have, "Mr. Klein died today, leaving a wife, two children, and a spacious three-bedroom apartment with a wood-burning fireplace."

Sally laughing. A nice moment.

HARRY   You know, the first time we met, I really didn't like you that much—

SALLY   *I* didn't like *you.*

HARRY   Yeah, you did. You were just so uptight then. You're much softer now.

SALLY   You know, I hate that kind of remark. It sounds like a compliment, but really it's an insult.

HARRY   Okay, you're still as hard as nails.

SALLY   I just didn't want to sleep with you, so you had to write it off as a character flaw instead of dealing with the possibility that it might have something to do with you.

HARRY   What's the statute of limitations on apologies?

SALLY   Ten years.

HARRY   Ooh. I can just get in under the wire.

Sally smiles, then after a beat, she makes the smallest of moves.

SALLY   Would you like to have dinner with me sometime?

HARRY   *(not knowing quite how to take this)*   Are we becoming friends now?

SALLY   Well,   *(this is not what she meant)*   yeah.

HARRY   Great. A woman friend. You know, you may be the first attractive woman I've not wanted to sleep with in my entire life.

SALLY *(slightly rejected)*   That's wonderful, Harry.

As they continue to walk along, we—

FADE OUT.

FADE IN:

DOCUMENTARY FOOTAGE
An OLDER COUPLE on a love seat.

FOURTH MAN   We were both born in the same hospital.

FOURTH WOMAN   *(overlaps)*   In 1921.

FOURTH MAN   Seven days apart.

FOURTH WOMAN   In the same hospital.

FOURTH MAN   We both grew up one block away from each other.

FOURTH WOMAN   *(overlaps)*   We both lived in tenements.

FOURTH MAN   On the Lower East Side.

FOURTH WOMAN   On Delancey Street.

FOURTH MAN   My family moved to the Bronx when I was ten.

FOURTH WOMAN   *(overlaps)*   He lived on Fordham Road.

FOURTH MAN   Hers moved when she was eleven.

FOURTH WOMAN   *(overlaps)*   I lived on 183rd Street.

FOURTH MAN   For six years she worked on the fifteenth floor—

FOURTH MAN	FOURTH WOMAN
—as a nurse where I had a practice on the fourteenth floor of the very same building.	I worked for a very prominent neurologist, Dr. Bemmelman.

FOURTH MAN	FOURTH WOMAN
We never met.	We never met. Can you imagine that?

FOURTH MAN   You know where we met? In an elevator—

FOURTH WOMAN   I was visiting family.

FOURTH MAN   —in the Ambassador Hotel in Chicago, Illinois.

FOURTH WOMAN   *(overlaps)*   He was on the third floor, I was on the twelfth.

FOURTH MAN   I rode up nine extra floors just to keep talking to her.

FOURTH WOMAN   Nine extra floors.

FADE OUT.

FADE IN:

A TIGHT SHOT of one of those toy felt birds that somehow is able to miraculously keep dunking its beak into a glass of water.

WIDER TO REVEAL:

INT. HARRY'S OFFICE—DAY
Harry is sitting in his office staring blankly at this ornithological phenomenon. As Harry stares, we hear the sound of a phone RING-ING. It is picked up by Sally.

SALLY   *(Voice-over)*   Hello.

HARRY   *(Voice-over)*   You sleeping?

SALLY   *(Voice-over)*   No, I was watching *Casablanca*.

HARRY   *(Voice-over)*   Channel, please.

SALLY   *(Voice-over)*   Eleven.

HARRY   *(Voice-over)*   Thank you. Got it.

As Harry continues to stare at the bird, we hear a few lines of dialogue from Casablanca: *"Of all the gin joints . . ." etc.*

As the Casablanca *dialogue continues, we—*

CUT TO:

INT. SALLY'S OFFICE—DAY
Sally is at her desk, doing business on the telephone. A woman walks in, hands her something.

HARRY *(Voice-over)* Now, you're telling me you would be happier with Victor Laszlo than with Humphrey Bogart?

The woman walks offscreen as Sally looks at the magazine on her desk, hangs up phone.

SALLY *(Voice-over)* When did I say that?

HARRY *(Voice-over)* When we drove to New York.

Sally turns to her computer terminal.

CUT TO:

INT. KOREAN GREENGROCERY—DAY
Sally moves along the salad bar, very selectively assembling a salad.

SALLY *(Voice-over)* I never said that. I would never have said that.

HARRY *(Voice-over)* All right, fine. Have it your way.

CUT TO:

INT. HARRY'S APARTMENT—DAY
Harry sits on the floor with a deck of cards, pitching them into a bowl.

HARRY *(Voice-over)* Have you been sleeping?

SALLY *(Voice-over)* Why?

HARRY *(Voice-over)* 'Cause I haven't been sleeping.

Harry continues pitching the cards. We see the room is bare except for a couple of chairs.

HARRY *(Voice-over)* (CONT'D)   I really miss Helen. Maybe I'm coming down with something. Last night I was up at four in the morning watching "Leave It to Beaver" in Spanish.

CUT TO:

INT. HARRY'S APARTMENT—DAY
Harry is sitting in a chair, trying to read a book. He has a thermometer in his mouth. He can't concentrate. He keeps reading the same paragraph over and over.

HARRY *(Voice-over)* (CONT'D)   *"Buenos días, Señora Cleaver. Dónde están Wallace y Theodore?"*

Finally, Harry flips to the last page and reads it.

HARRY *(Voice-over)* (CONT'D)   I'm not well.

CUT TO:

INT. FITNESS CLUB—DAY
Sally in a tap-dancing class.

SALLY *(Voice-over)*   Well, I went to bed at seven-thirty last night. I haven't done that since the third grade.

HARRY *(Voice-over)*   That's the good thing about depression. You get your rest.

SALLY *(Voice-over)*   I'm not depressed.

HARRY *(Voice-over)*   Okay, fine.

CUT TO:

EXT. CHINESE RESTAURANT—NIGHT
Through the window, we see Sally is going through a very detailed ordering session. The waiter's trying to keep up. Harry just stares.

HARRY *(Voice-over)*   Do you still sleep on the same side of the bed?

SALLY *(Voice-over)*   I did for a while, but now I'm pretty much using the whole bed.

HARRY   *(Voice-over)*   God, that's great. I feel weird when just my leg wanders over.

CUT TO:

EXT. STREET—DAY
Sally is putting mail into a mailbox, one letter at a time, checking to see that each letter has safely entered the box. Harry stands impatiently waiting.

HARRY   *(Voice-over)* (CONT'D)   I miss her.

SALLY   *(Voice-over)*   I don't miss him. I really don't.

HARRY   *(Voice-over)*   Not even a little?

Harry is getting impatient.

SALLY   *(Voice-over)*   You know what I miss? I miss the idea of him.

Harry moves around beside Sally and rests his elbow on top of the mailbox, watching incredulously as she continues the ritual.

HARRY   *(Voice-over)*   Maybe I only miss the idea of her. No, I miss the whole Helen.

Harry's impatience with Sally's letter mailing gets the best of him. He impulsively grabs the remaining letters in her hand, opens the box, shoves them in, then hustles her off.

SALLY   *(Voice-over)*   Last scene.

AND NOW SPLIT SCREEN:

INT. SALLY'S BEDROOM—NIGHT
Sally in bed on the phone watching Casablanca *on TV and talking to:*

INT. HARRY'S BEDROOM—NIGHT
Harry in bed on the phone watching Casablanca.

HARRY   Ingrid Bergman. Now *she's* low maintenance.

SALLY   Low maintenance?

HARRY   Yeah. There are two kinds of women: high maintenance and low maintenance.

SALLY   And Ingrid Bergman is low maintenance?

HARRY   An L.M. Definitely.

SALLY   Which am I?

HARRY   You're the worst kind. You're high maintenance, but you think you're low maintenance.

SALLY   I don't see that.

HARRY   You don't see that? *(mimicking her)* "Waiter, I'll begin with the house salad, but I don't want the regular dressing. I'll have the balsamic vinegar and oil, but on the side, and then the salmon with mustard sauce, but I want the mustard sauce on the side." "On the side" is a very big thing for you.

SALLY   Well, I just want it the way I want it.

HARRY   I know. High maintenance.

Sally smiling.

Bogart says, "Louie, this could be the beginning of a beautiful friendship."

HARRY (CONT'D)   Ooh. Best last line of a movie, ever.

As the movie ends.

HARRY (CONT'D)   I'm definitely coming down with something. Probably a twenty-four-hour tumor. They're going around.

SALLY   You don't have a tumor.

HARRY   How do you know?

SALLY   If you're so worried, go see a doctor.

HARRY   No, he'll just tell me it's nothing.

SALLY   Will you be able to sleep?

HARRY   If not, I'll be okay.

SALLY   What'll you do?

HARRY I'll stay up and moan. Maybe I should practice now.

He starts moaning.

SALLY Good night, Harry.

HARRY Good night.

They hang up. Harry remains in his place among the pillows on his bed. He moans again.

Sally turns off the light by her bed, and as she does, her side of the screen goes BLACK.

Another moan from Harry.

FADE OUT.

FADE IN:

EXT. STREET—DAY
Harry and Sally walking in front of pillars and a building.

HARRY I had my dream again. Where I'm making love, and the Olympic judges are watching. I've nailed the compulsories, so this is it. The finals. I get a 9.8 from the Canadian. I get a perfect 10 from the American. And my mother, disguised as an East German judge, gives me a 5.6. Must have been the dismount.

CUT TO:

EXT. CENTRAL PARK ARBOR—DAY
Harry and Sally in the park on a gorgeous fall day.

SALLY Basically it's the same one I've been having since I was twelve.

HARRY What happens?

SALLY No, it's too embarrassing.

HARRY Don't tell me.

SALLY Okay. There's this guy.

HARRY   What's he look like?

SALLY   I don't know. He's just kind of faceless.

HARRY   A faceless guy. Okay. Then what happens?

SALLY   He rips off my clothes.

HARRY   Then what happens?

SALLY   That's it.

HARRY   That's it? A faceless guy rips off your clothes. And that's the sex fantasy you've been having since you were twelve? Exactly the same?

SALLY   Well, sometimes I vary it a little.

HARRY   Which part?

SALLY   What I'm wearing.

Harry reacts.

SALLY (CONT'D)   What?

HARRY   Nothing.

                                                      CUT TO:

INT. METROPOLITAN MUSEUM—DUSK
Harry and Sally are walking through the Egyptian Temple exhibit.

HARRY   *(in a funny voice)*   I've decided that for the rest of the day we are going to talk like this.

SALLY   *(trying to imitate him)*   Like this.

HARRY   *(funny voice)*   No, please. To repeat after me. Pepper.

SALLY   *(trying to imitate)*   Pepper.

HARRY   *(funny voice)*   Pepper.

SALLY   *(laughing, still trying)*   Pepper.

HARRY   *(funny voice)*   Pepper.

SALLY   *(imitating)*   Pepper.

HARRY   *(funny voice)*   Pepper.

SALLY   *(imitating)*   Pepper.

HARRY   *(funny voice)*   Waiter, there is too much pepper on my paprikash.

SALLY   *(imitating)*   Waiter, there is too much pepper . . .

HARRY   *(funny voice)*   . . . there is too much pepper . . . on my paprikash.

SALLY   *(imitating)*   . . . on my paprikash.

HARRY   *(funny voice)*   But I would be proud to partake of your pecan pie.

Harry smiles, waits for her to repeat. Sally shakes her head.

HARRY (CONT'D)   *(funny voice)*   But I would be proud . . .

SALLY   *(imitating)*   But I would be proud . . .

HARRY   *(funny voice)*   . . . to partake . . .

SALLY   *(imitating)*   . . . to partake . . .

HARRY   *(funny voice)*   . . . of your pecan pie.

SALLY   *(imitating)*   . . . of your pecan pie.

HARRY   *(funny voice)*   Pecan pie.

SALLY   *(imitating)*   Pecan pie.

HARRY   *(funny voice)*   Pecan pie.

SALLY   *(imitating)*   Pecan pie.

HARRY   *(funny voice)*   Would you like to go to the movies with me tonight?

SALLY   *(imitating)*   Would . . . you . . . like . . . to go . . .

HARRY   *(funny voice)*   Not to repeat, please, to answer. Would you like to go to the movies . . . with me tonight?

SALLY *(in her regular voice)* Oh, oh, oh, I'd love to, Harry, but I can't.

HARRY *(still in funny voice)* What do you have, a hot date?

SALLY Well, yeah. Yeah.

HARRY *(in his regular voice)* Really?

SALLY Yeah, I was going to tell you, but . . . I don't know. I felt strange about it.

HARRY Why?

SALLY Well, because we've been spending so much time together . . .

HARRY Well, I think it's great you have a date.

SALLY You do?

HARRY Yeah. *(leaning in conspiratorially)* Is that what you're going to wear?

SALLY Yeah. Well, I don't know. Why?

HARRY I think you should wear skirts more. You look really good in skirts.

SALLY I do?

HARRY Yeah. You know, I have a theory that hieroglyphics are really an ancient comic strip about a character named Sphinxy.

SALLY You know, Harry, you should get out there, too.

HARRY *(in the funny voice again)* Oh, I'm not ready.

SALLY You should.

HARRY *(funny voice)* I would not be good for anybody right now.

SALLY It's time.

CUT TO:

INT. HARRY'S APARTMENT—DAY
Harry and Sally are unrolling a new rug.

HARRY   It was the most uncomfortable night of my life.

SALLY   Well, the first date back is always the toughest, Harry.

HARRY   You only had one date. How do you know it's not going to get worse?

SALLY   How much worse can it get than finishing dinner, having him reach over, pull a hair out of my head, and start flossing with it at the table?

HARRY   You're talking dream date compared to my horror. I started out fine, she's a very nice person, and we're sitting and we're talking in this Ethiopian restaurant she wanted to go to. I was making jokes, like, "Hey, I didn't know they had food in Ethiopia. This'll be a quick meal. I'll order two empty plates and we can leave." Nothing from her, not even a smile. So I downshift into small talk, and I ask her where she went to school and she says Michigan State and this reminds me of Helen. All of a sudden I'm in the middle of this massive anxiety attack, my heart's beating like a wild man, and I'm sweating like a pig.

SALLY   Helen went to Michigan State?

HARRY   No. She went to Northwestern. But they're both Big Ten schools.   *(beat)*   I was so upset, I had to leave the restaurant.

SALLY   Harry, I think it takes a long time. It might be months before we're actually able to enjoy going out with someone new.

HARRY   Yeah.

SALLY   And maybe even longer before we'll be actually able to go to bed with someone new.

HARRY   Oh, I went to bed with her.

SALLY   You went to bed with her?

HARRY   Sure.

SALLY   Oh.

CUT TO:

INT. BATTING CAGE IN QUEENS—DAY
Harry and Jess with bats in hand as the machine pitches.

JESS   I don't understand this relationship.

HARRY   What do you mean?

JESS   You enjoy being with her?

HARRY   Yeah.

JESS   You find her attractive?

HARRY   Yeah.

JESS   And you're not sleeping with her?

HARRY   No.

JESS   You're afraid to let yourself be happy.

HARRY   Why can't you give me credit for this? This is a big thing for me, I've never had a relationship with a woman that didn't involve sex. I feel like I'm growing.

One NINE-YEAR-OLD is waiting to use the batting cage and is watching Harry and Jess just stand there.

NINE-YEAR-OLD   Are you finished?

HARRY   I got a whole stack of quarters and I was here first.

NINE-YEAR-OLD   Were not.

HARRY Was too.

NINE-YEAR-OLD Were not.

HARRY Was too.

NINE-YEAR-OLD You jerk.

HARRY Creep. *(back to Jess)* Where was I?

JESS You were growing.

HARRY Yeah. It's very freeing. I can say anything to her.

JESS Are you saying you can say things to her you can't say to me?

HARRY No, it's just different. It's a whole different perspective. I get the woman's point of view on things. She tells me about the men she goes out with and I can talk to her about the women I see.

JESS You tell her about other women?

HARRY Yeah. Like the other night I made love to this woman and it was so incredible, I took her to a place that wasn't human. She actually meowed.

JESS You made a woman meow?

HARRY Yes. That's the point. I can say these things to her. And the great thing is, I don't have to lie because I'm not always thinking about how to get her into bed. I can just be myself.

JESS You made a woman meow?

CUT TO:

INT. CARNEGIE DELICATESSEN—DAY
Harry and Sally are seated at a table, waiting for their sandwiches.

SALLY What do you do with these women? Do you just get up out of bed and leave?

HARRY   Sure.

SALLY   Well, explain to me how you do it. What do you say?

A waiter brings their order.

HARRY   I say, I have an early meeting, an early haircut, an early squash game.

SALLY   You don't play squash.

HARRY   They don't know that. They just met me.

SALLY   *(rearranging the meat on her sandwich)*   That's disgusting.

HARRY   I know. I feel terrible.   *(takes a bite of sandwich)*

SALLY   You know, I am so glad I never got involved with you. I just would have ended up being some woman you had to get up out of bed and leave at three o'clock in the morning and go clean your andirons. And you don't even have a fireplace.   *(quite irritated now, slapping the meat over more quickly)*   Not that I would know this.

HARRY   Why are you getting so upset? This is not about you.

SALLY   Yes, it is. You're a human affront to all women. And I'm a woman.   *(bites into sandwich)*

HARRY   Hey, I don't feel great about this, but I don't hear anyone complaining.

SALLY   Of course not. You're out the door too fast.

HARRY   I think they have an okay time.

SALLY   How do you know?

HARRY   What do you mean, how do I know? I know.

SALLY   Because they . . . ?   *(she makes a gesture with her hands)*

HARRY   Yes, because they . . .   *(he makes the same gesture back)*

SALLY   How do you know they're really . . .   *(she makes the same gesture)*

HARRY   What are you saying, they fake orgasm?

SALLY   It's possible.

HARRY   Get outta here.

SALLY   Why? Most women, at one time or another, have faked it.

HARRY   Well, they haven't faked it with me.

SALLY   How do you know?

HARRY   Because I know.

SALLY   Oh right.   *(sets her sandwich down)*   That's right. I forgot. You're a man.

HARRY   What's that supposed to mean?

SALLY   Nothing. It's just that all men are sure it never happens to them, and most women at one time or another have done it, so you do the math.

HARRY   You don't think I can tell the difference?

SALLY   No.

HARRY   Get outta here.

Harry bites into his sandwich. Sally just stares at him. A seductive look comes onto her face.

SALLY   Oooh!

Harry, sandwich in hand, chewing his food, looks up at Sally.

SALLY (CONT'D)   Oh! Oooh!

HARRY   Are you okay?

Sally, her eyes closed, ruffles her hair seductively.

SALLY Oh, God!

Harry is beginning to figure out what Sally is doing.

SALLY (CONT'D) Oooh! Oh, God!

Sally tilts her head back.

SALLY (CONT'D) Oh!

Her eyes closed, she runs her hand over her face, down her neck.

SALLY (CONT'D) Oh, my God! Oh, yeah, right there.

Harry looks around, noticing that others in the deli are noticing Sally. She's really making a show now.

SALLY (CONT'D) *(gasps)* Oh!

A man in the background turns to look at her.

SALLY (CONT'D) Oh! Oh! *(gasps)* Oh God! Oh! Yes!

Harry, embarrassed, stares at her in disbelief.

SALLY (CONT'D) *(pounding the table)* Yes! Yes!

The man in the background is now watching intently.

SALLY (CONT'D) *(pounding the table with both hands)* Yes! Yes! Yes!

Harry looks around, very embarrassed, smiles at customers. An OLDER WOMAN seated nearby stares.

SALLY (CONT'D) Yes! Yes!

By now, the place is totally silent and everyone is watching.

SALLY (CONT'D) Yes! Oh! *(still thumping table)* Yes, yes, yes!

Sally leans her head back, as though experiencing the final ecstatic convulsions of an orgasm.

SALLY (CONT'D) Yes! Yes! Yes!

She finally tosses her head forward.

SALLY (CONT'D) Oh. Oh. Oh.

Sally sinks down into her chair, tousling her hair, rubbing her hand down her neck to her chest.

SALLY (CONT'D) Oh, God.

Then, suddenly, the act is over. Sally calmly picks up her fork, digs into her coleslaw, and smiles innocently at Harry.

A waiter approaches the Older Woman to take her food order. The woman looks at him.

OLDER WOMAN I'll have what she's having.

FADE OUT.

FADE IN:

EXT. CENTRAL PARK—DAY
Various scenes of the snow-blanketed park: A horse pulls a carriage; people bundled up in winter clothing walk along the snow-covered paths; and a lone cross-country skier crosses a large expanse.

CUT TO:

EXT. ROCKEFELLER PLAZA—NIGHT
The huge Christmas tree in the square, a woman skating expertly in the center of the ice rink.

CUT TO:

EXT. STREET—NIGHT
A store window with a Christmas display, families admiring it.

CUT TO:

EXT. PARK—DAY
Children riding sleds and toboggans down a hill.

CUT TO:

EXT. STREET—NIGHT
Pedestrians, huddled against the cold, walking by lighted Christmas trees.

CUT TO:

EXT. PARK—DAY
The Wollman rink, full of skaters. A man walks his dog outside the fence.

CUT TO:

EXT. CHRISTMAS TREE LOT—DAY
Sally is paying for a tree. Then she and Harry pick it up, he holding the top and she the bottom, and carry it to Sally's. Together.

CUT TO:

INT. NEW YEAR'S EVE PARTY—NIGHT
Champagne is popped.

We know it's New Year's Eve because people are wearing funny hats and there's one of those mirrored things hanging from the ceiling and casting twinkle lights on a fairly large crowd of revelers in a penthouse apartment somewhere in Manhattan.

A band is PLAYING. Harry and Sally are dancing.

He dips her.

SALLY I really want to thank you for taking me out tonight.

HARRY Oh, don't be silly. And next year, if neither of us is with somebody, you've got a date.

SALLY Deal. See, now we can dance cheek to cheek.

They dance a moment and then the MUSIC ENDS. They go on dancing a bit longer and for a split second we see the beginnings of something . . . an inkling . . . a little tender moment. Then—

VOICE *(Offscreen)* Hey, everybody, ten seconds to the New Year!

The CROWD begins to count down:

CROWD Ten, nine . . .

HARRY Want to get some air?

SALLY Yeah.

CROWD . . . eight, seven, six . . .

EXT. NEW YEAR'S EVE PARTY—NIGHT

CROWD (CONT'D) . . . five, four . . .

Harry and Sally go out onto the balcony.

CROWD (CONT'D) . . . three, two, Happy New Year!

All around Harry and Sally, couples are hugging, kissing, celebrating. It is slightly uncomfortable.

HARRY Happy New Year.

SALLY Happy New Year.

They kiss quickly and awkwardly.

FADE OUT.

FADE IN:

DOCUMENTARY FOOTAGE
A COUPLE on a love seat.

FIFTH WOMAN He was the head counselor at the boys' camp, and I was the head counselor at the girls' camp. They had a social one night. *(beat)* And he walked across the room. I thought he was coming to talk to my friend Maxine, because people were always walking across rooms to talk to Maxine, but he was coming to talk to me. And he said—

FIFTH MAN I'm Ben Small of the Coney Island Smalls.

FIFTH WOMAN And at that moment, I knew, I knew the way you know about a good melon.

FADE OUT.

FADE IN:

> EXT. WEST BROADWAY, NEAR RESTAURANT—EARLY EVENING
> Sally and her friend Marie walking down the street on their way to
> a restaurant.

SALLY   You sent flowers to yourself?

MARIE   Sixty dollars I spend on this big stupid arrangement of flowers, and I wrote a card that I planned to leave out on the front table where Arthur would just happen to see it—

SALLY   What did the card say?

MARIE   "Please say yes. Love, Jonathan."

SALLY   Did it work?

MARIE   He never even came over. He forgot this charity thing that his wife was chairman of.
(beat)   He's never going to leave her.

SALLY   Of course he isn't.

MARIE   You're right, you're right. I know you're right.   *(beat)*   Where is this place?

SALLY   Somewhere in the next block.

MARIE   Oh, I can't believe I'm doing this.

SALLY   Look, Harry is one of my best friends, and you are one of my best friends, and if by some chance you two hit it off, we could all still be friends instead of drifting apart the way you do when you get involved with someone who doesn't know your friends.

MARIE   You and I haven't drifted apart since I started seeing Arthur.

SALLY   If Arthur ever left his wife and I actually met him, I'm sure you and I would drift apart.

MARIE   He's never going to leave her.

SALLY   Of course he isn't.

MARIE   You're right, you're right, I know you're right.

CUT TO:

EXT. WEST BROADWAY, NEAR RESTAURANT—NIGHT
Harry and his friend Jess coming down the street.

JESS   I don't know about this.

HARRY   It's just a dinner.

JESS   You know, I've finally gotten to a place in my life where I'm comfortable with the fact that it's just me and my work.   *(they walk on)*   If she's so great, why aren't *you* taking her out?

HARRY   How many times do I have to tell you, we're just friends.

JESS   So you're saying she's not that attractive?

HARRY   No, I told you she is attractive.

JESS   But you also said she had a good personality.

HARRY   She has a good personality.

Jess makes a "precisely my point" gesture.

HARRY (CONT'D)   What?

JESS   When someone's not attractive, they're always described as having a good personality.

HARRY   Look. If you had asked me what does she look like and I said, she has a good personality, *that* means she's not attractive. But just because I happen to mention she has a good personality, she could be either. She could be attractive with a good personality, or not attractive with a good personality.

JESS   So which one is she?

HARRY   Attractive.

JESS   But not beautiful, right?

Harry glares at him.

CUT TO:

INT. RESTAURANT—NIGHT

Harry, Jess, Sally, and Marie at a table. A waiter has just brought them drinks. It is clear from the arrangement at the table that Harry is meant to be with Marie and Jess is meant to be with Sally. Jess and Sally are talking to each other, while Harry and Marie carry on their own conversation.

JESS   *(to Sally)*   It's like whenever I read Jimmy Breslin, it's as if he's leaving some kind of wake-up call for the city of New York.

SALLY   What do you mean by a wake-up call?

They continue talking as we now focus on Harry and Marie's conversation:

HARRY   Would I have seen any of your windows?

MARIE   Well, just a couple of weeks ago, I did a thing with hostages.

HARRY   Oh, the thing with people in blindfolds.

Back to Jess and Sally, who obviously is not enjoying or agreeing with what he is saying.

SALLY   *(to Jess)*   Uh, let's just say I'm . . . I'm really not a big fan of Jimmy Breslin.

JESS   Well, he's the reason I became a writer, but that's not important.

A little pause.

SALLY   Harry, you and Marie are both from New Jersey.

MARIE   Really?

HARRY   Where are you from?

MARIE   South Orange.

HARRY   Haddonfield.

MARIE   Oh.

They all look at each other.

Then they look at their menus.

HARRY   So what are we going to order?

SALLY   I'm going to start with the grilled radicchio.

HARRY   Jess, Sally is a great orderer. Not only does she always pick the best thing on the menu, but she orders it in a way that even the chef didn't know how good it would be.

Sally shoots Harry a look.

JESS   I think restaurants have become too important.

MARIE   Oh, I agree. "Restaurants are to people in the eighties what theater was to people in the sixties." I read that in a magazine.

JESS   I wrote that.

MARIE   Get outta here.

JESS   No, I did. I wrote that.

MARIE   I never quoted anything from a magazine in my life. That's amazing. Don't you think that's amazing? And you wrote it?

JESS   I also wrote, "Pesto is the quiche of the eighties."

MARIE   Get over yourself.

JESS   I did.

MARIE   Where did I read that?

JESS *New York* magazine.

HARRY Sally writes for *New York* magazine.

MARIE Do you know, that piece had a real impact on me. I don't know that much about writing, but . . .

JESS Look, it spoke to you, and that pleases me.

MARIE It had a wonderful, unique—is the word "style"?

JESS If you say that's the word, that's the word.

MARIE I . . . I mean . . . I really have to admire people who can be as . . . as . . . articulate . . .

JESS Nobody's ever quoted me back to me before.

CUT TO:

EXT. WEST BROADWAY—NIGHT
Harry, Jess, Marie, and Sally are walking up the avenue, all four of them in a row, ad-libbing about the meal and what a nice night it is. They walk past a shoe store, and Marie suddenly yanks Sally over.

MARIE Oooo, I've been looking for a red suede pump. *(beat)* What do you think of Jess?

The two men keep walking.

SALLY Well, uh . . .

MARIE *(interrupting)* Do you think you could go out with him?

SALLY I don't know . . .

MARIE —because I feel really comfortable with him.

SALLY You want to go out with Jess?

MARIE If it's all right with you.

SALLY Sure. Sure. I'm just worried about Harry. He's very sensitive, he's going through a rough period, and I just don't want you to reject him right now.

MARIE   I wouldn't. I totally understand.

SALLY   Okay.

EXT. WEST BROADWAY—NIGHT
Harry and Jess apparently in the midst of an identical conversation.
They're stopped in front of a running-equipment store.

JESS   If you don't think you're going to call Marie, do you mind if I call her?

HARRY   No.

JESS   Good, good.

HARRY   But for tonight you shouldn't . . . I mean, Sally's very vulnerable right now. I mean, you can call Marie, it's fine, but just, like, wait a week or so, you know? Don't make any moves tonight.

JESS   Fine. No problem. I wasn't even thinking about tonight.

The women join them.

JESS (CONT'D)   Well.   *(beat)*   I don't feel like walking anymore, I think I'll get a cab.

MARIE   I'll go with you.

JESS   Great.   *(he leaps into the street as he spots a cab)*   Taxi!

The cab SCREECHES to a halt, and Jess and Marie get into it and it pulls away, leaving Sally and Harry on the curb.

FADE OUT.

FADE IN:

DOCUMENTARY FOOTAGE
Another OLDER COUPLE, both Asian, sitting together on the love seat.

ASIAN MAN   A man came to me and said, "I found nice girl for you. She lives in the next village, and she is ready for marriage." We were not supposed to meet until the wedding. But I wanted to make sure, so I sneaked into her village and hid behind a tree and watched her wash the clothes. I think, if I don't like the way she looks, I don't marry her. But she looked really nice to me. So I said okay to the man, we get married. We are married for fifty-five years.

                                            FADE OUT.

FADE IN:

> EXT. THE SHARPER IMAGE—DAY—ESTABLISHING

> INT. THE SHARPER IMAGE—DAY
> *One of those places with gifts for people who have everything. Harry and Sally are browsing through. He shoots a basketball into a mini-sized hoop.*

HARRY   I have to get this, I have to.

SALLY   Harry, we're here for Jess and Marie.

HARRY   I know we'll find them something, there's great stuff here.

SALLY   We should've gone to the plant store.

> *He picks up a pith helmet with a battery-operated fan in it and puts it on Sally's head.*

HARRY   Here. Perfect for them.

SALLY   What's that?

HARRY   Battery-operated pith helmet, with fan.

SALLY   Why is this necessary in life?

HARRY   I don't know. Look, look at this. *(indicating fan)* It also makes great fries.

> *He spots something across the aisle.*

HARRY (CONT'D)   Oh, oh, oh.

> *He heads toward it.*

HARRY (CONT'D)   Good. Call off the dogs. The hunt is over.

He goes to one of those machines that allow you to sing the lead to the backup vocal and instrumental on a song.

HARRY (CONT'D)   Sally, this is the greatest. *(into the microphone)* Sally, please report to me. Look at this. This is incredible. They're gonna love this. This is a singing machine.

Harry puts in one of the cassettes. The INSTRUMENTAL for "The Surrey with the Fringe on Top" comes on.

HARRY (CONT'D)   Look. You sing the lead, and this has the backup and everything. This is from *Oklahoma!* Here's the lyrics right here.

SALLY   *(reading)*   "Surrey with the Fringe on Top."

HARRY   Yeah, this is perfect.

He starts singing giddily.

HARRY (CONT'D)   "Chicks and ducks and geese better scurry,
When I take you out in the surrey,
When I take you out in the surrey
With the fringe on top."   *(pointing to Sally)*   Now you.

She starts to sing.

SALLY   *(singing)*   "Watch that fringe and . . ."

Harry resumes singing, too, as the absurd and dizzy instrumental continues. They both get more and more idiotic.

HARRY AND SALLY   *(singing)*   ". . . see how it flutters,
When I drive them high steppin' strutters,
Nosey pokes'll peek through their shutters and their eyes will pop!"

Suddenly Harry turns pale and stops singing.

SALLY   *(continuing to sing)*   "The wheels are yeller, the upholstery's brown,
The dashboard's gen-u-ine leather
With isinglass curtains y'can roll . . ."

Sally notices something's wrong.

The backup MUSIC CONTINUES as she stops, too.

SALLY (CONT'D)   What? It's my voice, isn't it? You hate my voice. I know it's terrible. Joe hated it. . . .

HARRY   It's Helen.

SALLY   Helen?

HARRY   She's coming right toward me.

The BACKUP VOCAL CONTINUES, as we see coming toward Harry a dark-haired, very chic woman, HELEN, accompanied by a tall, attractive man, IRA.

HELEN   How are you, Harry?

HARRY   *(he swallows)*   Fine. I'm fine.

HELEN   This is Ira Stone. Harry Burns.

IRA   Harry.

They shake hands. It's very awkward. Harry suddenly remembers Sally.

HARRY   I'm sorry. This is Sally Albright. Helen Hillson and Ira.

IRA   Sally.

HELEN   Nice to meet you.

SALLY   Hi.

A terrible moment.

HELEN   Well, see you.

HARRY   Yeah. Nice to meet you, Ira.

A smile, and they move on. HOLD on Harry, about to faint.

SALLY   You okay?

HARRY   Yeah, I'm perfect.

Harry looks like one of those cartoon characters who's been struck on the head with a mallet.

HARRY (CONT'D)   She looked weird, didn't she? She looked really weird. She looked very weird.

SALLY   I've never seen her before.

HARRY   Trust me, she looked weird. Her legs looked heavy. Really, she must be retaining water.

SALLY   Harry.

HARRY   Believe me, the woman saved everything.

CUT TO:

EXT. PLANT SHOP—DAY
Sally is paying for a plant. Harry is just staring blankly into a ficus. Sally approaches.

SALLY   You sure you're okay?

HARRY   Oh, I'm fine. Look, it had to happen at some point. In a city of eight million people you're bound to run into your ex-wife. So, boom, it happened. And now I'm fine.

CUT TO:

INT. JESS AND MARIE'S APARTMENT—DAY
A nice West Side floor-through with a beautiful fireplace and a great deal of furniture—about twice as much furniture as is necessary, as a matter of fact.

Marie and Jess in sneakers, jeans, baggy shirts, are clearly in the middle of some sort of dispute. Harry is still distracted. There are a few unpacked boxes—some books, a couple of ashtrays, a glass, etc.

JESS   It works. I like it. It says home to me.

MARIE   *(to Jess)*   Okay, okay, we'll let Harry and Sally be the judge.   *(to Sally and Harry)*   What do *you* think?

Marie points to a large wagon wheel that's been made into a coffee table with a round plate of glass over it.

Harry looks at Jess, who's glaring at him.

HARRY   It's nice.

JESS   Case closed.

Jess smiles, victorious.

MARIE   Of course he likes it. He's a guy. Sally?

Sally crinkles up her nose.

JESS   What's so awful about it?

MARIE   It's so awful there's no way even to begin to explain what is so awful about it.

JESS   Honey, I don't object to any of *your* things.

MARIE   If we had an extra room, we could put all your things in it, including your bar stools, and . . .

JESS   Wait, wait, honey, honey, wait, wait. You don't like my bar stools?

Marie looks at him. Of course she doesn't like his bar stools.

Jess turns to Harry for help.

Harry, we now see, has wandered away and stands by the window and he's staring out like a forlorn figure in a Magritte painting.

JESS   Harry, come on.   *(beat)*   Someone has to be on my side.

No response from Harry.

MARIE   I'm on your side. I'm just trying to help you have good taste.

JESS   I have good taste.

MARIE   Everybody thinks they have good taste and a sense of humor, but they couldn't possibly all.

Harry stands up, looks around the room.

HARRY   You know, it's funny—we started out like this, Helen and I. We had blank walls. We hung things. We picked out tiles together. Then you know what happens? Six years later you find yourself singing "Surrey with the Fringe on Top" in front of Ira.

SALLY   Do we have to talk about this right now?

HARRY   Yes, I think that right now is actually the perfect time to talk about this, because I want our friends to benefit from the wisdom of my experience.   *(he's becoming more and more upset)*   Right now everything is great. Everyone is happy. Everyone is in love. And that's wonderful. But you gotta know that sooner or later you're gonna be screaming at each other about who's gonna get this dish.   *(he picks up a cracked ashtray)*   This eight-dollar dish will cost you a thousand dollars in phone calls to the legal firm of "That's mine, this is yours."

SALLY   Harry—

HARRY   *(to Sally)*   Please.   *(to Jess and Marie)*   Jess, Marie, do me a favor. For your own good. *Put your name in your books.* Right now. Before they get mixed up and you don't know whose is whose. Because someday, believe it or not, you'll go fifteen rounds over who's going to get this coffee table, this stupid wagon-wheel, Roy Rogers, garage-sale coffee table.

JESS   I thought you liked it.

HARRY   *(still shouting)*   I was being nice.

Harry slams out the door.

Sally looks at Jess and Marie.

SALLY   He just bumped into Helen.

Sally goes out the door, leaving Jess and Marie.

MARIE   I want you to know that I will never want that wagon-wheel coffee table.

CUT TO:

EXT. JESS AND MARIE'S APARTMENT—DAY
Harry is sitting on the stoop. Sally comes down the steps.

HARRY   I know, I know. I shouldn't have done that.

SALLY   Harry, you're going to have to try and find a way of not expressing every feeling that you have every moment that you have them.

HARRY   Oh, really.

SALLY   Yes. There are times and places for things.

HARRY   Well, the next time you're giving a lecture series in social graces, would you let me know, 'cause I'll sign up.

SALLY   You don't have to take your anger out on me.

HARRY   Oh, I think I'm entitled to throw a little anger your way. Especially when I'm being told how to live my life by Miss Hospital Corners.

SALLY   What is that supposed to mean?

HARRY   I mean, nothing bothers you. You never get upset about anything.

SALLY   Don't be ridiculous.

HARRY   What? You never get upset about Joe. I never

see that back up on you. How is that possible? Don't you experience any feelings of loss?

SALLY   I don't have to take this crap from you.

Sally storms back to the building. Harry follows.

HARRY   If you're so over Joe, why aren't you seeing anyone?

SALLY   I see people.

HARRY   See people? Have you slept with *one* person since you broke up with Joe?

SALLY   What the hell does that have to do with anything? That will prove that I'm over Joe? Because I fuck somebody? Harry, you're going to have to move back to New Jersey because you've slept with everybody in New York, and I don't see that turning Helen into a faint memory for you. Besides, I will make love to someone when it's making love, not the way you do it, like you're out for revenge or something.

HARRY   Are you finished now?

SALLY   Yes.

HARRY   Can I say something?

SALLY   Yes.

HARRY   I'm sorry.

He walks over and gives her a hug.

They walk back up the steps toward the house. Jess passes them, coming down the stairs carrying out the wagon-wheel coffee table.

JESS   Don't say a word.

                                                                    CUT TO:

INT. JESS AND MARIE'S APARTMENT—NIGHT
It's all furnished now, very comfortable, not lavish. A corduroy couch, lots of books and records, a couple of quilts hanging over the backs of

chairs. No wagon-wheel coffee table. A game of Win, Lose or Draw is in progress. Sally's team consists of Harry, Alice, and Jess. EMILY, Harry's date, is snuggled up against him. Alice's husband, GARY, Marie, and JULIAN, Sally's date, are part of the other team.

Sally is feverishly drawing what is supposed to be a baby.

JESS It's a monkey. It's a monkey. Monkey see, monkey do.

Sally shakes her head no and keeps drawing.

JESS (CONT'D) It's an ape. Going ape.

ALICE It's a baby.

Sally nods yes.

JESS *Planet of the Apes.*

Sally writes the word "BABY" on the paper. She continues to draw what looks like a big mouth.

HARRY *Planet of the Apes.* She just said it's a baby. How about planet of the dopes?

JESS It doesn't look like a baby.

Sally now has drawn what looks like arrows on lines coming out of the mouth.

HARRY It's a big-mouth baby. Mick Jagger as a baby.

JESS Baby ape! Baby ape!

ALICE Baby's breath.

HARRY *(overlap)* Rosemary's Baby's mouth.

JESS "Won't you come home, Bill Baby?"

ALICE *(overlap)* Kiss the baby!

HARRY Melancholy Baby's mouth!

JESS Baby fish mouth!

JULIAN Fifteen seconds.

ALICE Baby boom!

Sally is getting frustrated, can do nothing but draw more arrows out of the mouth.

JESS   Draw something resembling anything!

ALICE   . . . Kiss the baby . . .

HARRY   *(overlap)*   Baby spitting up. Exorcist baby!

ALICE   "Yes, sir, that's my baby."

HARRY   "No, sir, don't mean maybe."

JULIAN   That's it. Time's up.

SALLY   Baby talk.

JESS   Baby talk? What's that? That's not a saying.

HARRY   Oh, but "baby fish mouth" is sweeping the nation.

GARY   Final score: our team, 110, you guys, 60.

SALLY   *(to Julian)*   I can't draw.

JULIAN   No. That's a baby, and that's a baby talking. You're wonderful.

He puts his arms around her.

MARIE   All right, who wants coffee?

Sally and Julian kiss. Harry looks on.

JESS   I do, and I love you.

ALICE   Do you have any tea?

MARIE   One tea.

Harry holds up his hand.

HARRY   Industrial strength.

EMILY   I'll have tea also.

SALLY   I'll help you.   *(to Julian)*   Decaf?

JULIAN   Yeah.

ALICE   Cream.

EMILY *(to Marie)* Where's the bathroom?

MARIE Through that door, down the hall.

Emily and Harry kiss as she heads away. Sally notices this.

Jess and Julian are at the drawing board, examining Sally's "baby" drawing.

JESS Never looked like a baby to me.

JULIAN Which part?

JESS All of it.

HARRY Hey, Jess, you were going to show me the cover art for your book.

JESS Oh, yeah, yeah. It's in the den. *(to Julian)* Look, uh, Julian, help yourself—have some more wine, whatever you like, okay? *(to Harry)* I like saying it's in the den. It's got a nice ring to it.

INT. KITCHEN—NIGHT

Sally and Marie go about getting the coffee ready.

SALLY Emily's a little young for Harry, don't you think?

MARIE Well, she's young, but look what she's done.

SALLY What has she done? She makes desserts.

INT. DEN—NIGHT

HARRY Does Julian seem a little stuffy to you?

JESS He's a good guy. You should talk to him, get to know him.

HARRY He's too tall to talk to.

INT. KITCHEN—NIGHT

MARIE She makes 3,500 chocolate mousse pies a week.

SALLY Emily is *Aunt* Emily?

INT. DEN—NIGHT

JESS   He took us all to a Mets game last week. It was great.

HARRY   You all went to a Mets game together?

JESS   It was a last-minute thing.

HARRY   But Sally hates baseball.

INT. KITCHEN—NIGHT

SALLY   Harry doesn't even like sweets.

MARIE   Julian is great.

SALLY   I know. He's a grown-up.

INT. DEN—NIGHT

JESS   Emily is terrific.

HARRY   Yeah. Of course, when I asked her where she was when Kennedy was shot, she said, "Ted Kennedy was shot?"

JESS   No.

CUT TO:

INT. HARRY'S BEDROOM—NIGHT
Harry in bed reading, trying not to look at the last page, but finally he can't help himself. As he flips to the last page, the phone RINGS. He reaches for the phone and answers it.

HARRY   Hello.

SALLY   *(through filter)*   Are you alone?

HARRY   Yeah. I was just finishing a book.

SALLY   *(through filter)*   Could you come over?

HARRY   What's the matter?

INT. SALLY'S BEDROOM—NIGHT

SALLY   He's getting married.

HARRY   *(through filter)*   Who?

SALLY   Joe.

INT. HARRY'S BEDROOM—NIGHT

HARRY   I'll be right there.

CUT TO:

INT. HALLWAY OUTSIDE SALLY'S APARTMENT—NIGHT
Sally opens the door. She wears a bathrobe. She is crying and looks terrible.

SALLY   Hi.

HARRY   Are you all right?

SALLY   Come on in.

Harry follows her inside and closes the door.

INT. SALLY'S APARTMENT—NIGHT

SALLY   *(through tears)*   I'm sorry to call you so late.

HARRY   It's all right.

She goes on sobbing, then pulls back and gives a huge wheeze.

SALLY   I need a Kleenex.

HARRY   Okay.

SALLY   Okay.

Sally starts into the bedroom.

INT. SALLY'S BEDROOM—NIGHT
Sally enters the room, looks for the Kleenex. Harry sits on the bed.

SALLY   He just called me up. Just wanted to see how you were. Fine, how are you? Fine. . . . His secretary's on vacation, everything's all backed up, he's got a big case in Newark, blah blah blah, and I'm thinking, I'm over him, I really am over him, I can't believe I was ever remotely interested in any of this, and then he said, "I have some news."

Sally starts to cry again.

SALLY (CONT'D) She works in his office. She's a paralegal. Her name is Kimberly. *He just met her.* She's supposed to be his transitional person, she's not supposed to be the one. *(beat)* All this time I've been saying he didn't want to get married. *(beat)* But the truth is he didn't want to marry *me*. He didn't love *me*.

HARRY If you could take him back right now, would you?

SALLY No. But why didn't he want to marry me? What's the matter with me?

HARRY Nothing.

SALLY I'm difficult.

HARRY You're challenging.

SALLY I'm too structured. I'm completely closed off.

HARRY But in a good way.

SALLY No, no, no. I drove him away.

Crying even harder now.

SALLY (CONT'D) And I'm going to be forty.

HARRY When?

SALLY Someday.

HARRY In eight years.

SALLY But it's there, it's just sitting there like this big dead end. It's not the same for men. Charlie Chaplin had babies when he was seventy-three.

HARRY Yeah, but he was too old to pick them up.

She smiles a little, then starts crying again.

HARRY (CONT'D) Oh, c'mere, c'mere. *(he gives her a*

hug) It's going to be okay. You're gonna be fine, you'll see.

Sally sniffles into Harry's shirt.

HARRY (CONT'D)   Go ahead, it's not one of my favorites anyway. It's gonna be okay.

Harry holds her. He gives her a kiss, starts to break the hug.

HARRY (CONT'D)   I'll make you some tea.

SALLY   Harry, could you just hold me a little longer?

HARRY   Oh, sure. There.

Harry holds her. After a beat, Sally looks up at him, almost searching for something. She kisses him. A hungry, needy kiss. Harry is caught slightly off guard, but returns the kiss. As they begin to make love—

> CUT TO:

INT. SALLY'S BEDROOM—LATER
They've made love. Both of them lying in bed, Sally is in Harry's arms. Sally has a smile on her face. Harry stares straight ahead.

SALLY   Are you comfortable?

Harry nods.

HARRY   Sure.

After a pause.

SALLY   Do you want something to drink or something?

HARRY   No, I'm okay.

SALLY   *(getting up)*   Well, I'm going to get up for some water, so it's really no trouble.

HARRY   Okay. Water.

INT. KITCHEN—NIGHT
Sally enters and gets a bottle of water from the refrigerator. She goes to the cabinet and takes out two glasses and pours.

INT. BEDROOM—NIGHT

Harry lying in Sally's bed, still staring straight ahead. Finally, he looks around and reaches for a file box he sees. He opens it and looks inside.

INT. KITCHEN—NIGHT

As Sally stands thinking, a little smile on her face.

INT. BEDROOM—NIGHT

Harry is sitting up in bed with the light on, looking through the box of index cards.

Sally comes in with the glasses of water.

HARRY *(looking up from the box)* You have all your videotapes alphabetized and on index cards.

Sally hands him the water.

HARRY (CONT'D) Thank you.

A silence while Harry desultorily goes through the box.

Unbelievably awkward.

Every SOUND is louder than it actually is. The riffle of the index cards. Sally taking a gulp of water. Harry rearranging his pillow.

SALLY Do you want to watch something?

HARRY No, not unless you do.

SALLY No, that's okay.

A pause. He puts the file box back. Sally slides back into bed, nestles into his shoulder.

SALLY (CONT'D) Do you want to go to sleep?

HARRY Okay.

She turns off the lamp and settles in beside Harry.

CUT TO:

INT. BEDROOM—DAY

Sally wakes up. Sees the other half of the bed empty. Where's Harry? She turns over and sees him getting dressed.

SALLY   Where are you going?

HARRY   I gotta go.

Sally stares at him.

HARRY (CONT'D)   I gotta go home, I gotta change my clothes, and then I have to go to work and so do you, but after work I'd like to take you out to dinner if you're free. Are you free?

SALLY   Yes.

HARRY   Fine. I'll call you later.

SALLY   Fine.

HARRY   Fine.

Harry gives her a little kiss, walks out.

HOLD on her in bed as the door SLAMS.

Next to her is the phone.

INT. JESS AND MARIE'S BEDROOM—MORNING

A bed with a phone on each side. Jess and Marie asleep in bed.

The phone on Marie's side of the bed starts to RING. Marie and Jess both wake up, look at the clock. They can't believe how early it is.

It RINGS again.

JESS   *(accusingly)*   Yours.

Marie picks up the phone, pulls the phone onto the bed.

MARIE   Hello.

WIPE IN FROM RIGHT:

Sally sitting up in bed, talking on phone.

SALLY   I'm sorry to call so early—

MARIE   Are you all right?

JESS   No one I know would call at this hour.

The phone RINGS on Jess's side of the bed.

SALLY   I did something terrible.

Jess picks up the phone.

MARIE   What did you do?

WIPE IN FROM LEFT:

Harry standing at public phone. Now we see all four of them on-screen, Marie and Jess in their bed on their phones, talking to Sally in her apartment at the far right, and Harry on a pay phone in the street at the far left.

JESS   *(into phone)*   No one I know would call at this hour.

SALLY   It's so awful.

HARRY   I need to talk.

MARIE   What happened?

JESS   What's the matter?

SALLY   Harry came over last night . . .

HARRY   I went over to Sally's last night . . .

SALLY   . . . because I was upset that Joe was getting married . . .

HARRY   . . . and one thing led to another . . .

SALLY   . . . and before I knew it, we were kissing . . . and then . . .   *(she shakes her head in horror, remembering)*

HARRY   . . . to make a long story short . . .

SALLY	HARRY
We did it.	We did it.

JESS	MARIE
(whispering to Marie)	*(whispering to Jess)*
They did it.	They did it.

MARIE   *(back to Sally)*   That's great, Sally.

JESS   *(back to Harry)*   We've been praying for it.

MARIE   You should have done it in the first place.

JESS   For months we've been saying, you should do it.

MARIE   You guys belong together.

JESS   It's like killing two birds with one stone.

MARIE   It's like two wrongs make a right.

| JESS | MARIE |
| How was it? | How was it? |

HARRY   The during part was good . . .

SALLY   I thought it was good . . .

HARRY   . . . but then I felt suffocated.

SALLY   . . . but then I guess it wasn't.

JESS   Jesus, I'm sorry.

MARIE   The worst.

HARRY   I just wanted to get out of there.

SALLY   He just disappeared.

HARRY   I feel so bad.

SALLY   I'm so embarrassed.

JESS   I don't blame you.

MARIE   That's horrible.

HARRY   I think I'm coming down with something.

SALLY   I think I'm catching a cold.

JESS   Look, it would have been great if it had worked out, but it didn't.

MARIE   You should never go to bed with anyone when you've found out your last boyfriend is getting married.

HARRY   Who's that talking?

JESS   Who?

SALLY   Is that Jess on the phone?

JESS   It's Jane Fonda on the VCR.

MARIE   It's Bryant Gumbel.

JESS	MARIE
Do you want to come over for breakfast?	Do you want to come over for breakfast?

Marie and Jess look at each other, horrified.

HARRY   No, I'm not up to it.

SALLY   No, I feel too awful.

JESS	MARIE
Good.	Good.

MARIE   I mean, it's so early.

JESS   Call me later if you want.

MARIE   I'll call you later, okay?

HARRY   Okay, bye.

SALLY   Bye.

JESS   Bye.

MARIE   Bye.

Everyone hangs up. Harry and Sally frames WIPE OFFSCREEN LEFT AND RIGHT, leaving Jess and Marie on-screen.

HOLD on Marie and Jess.

Marie looks at Jess.

MARIE   God.

JESS   I know.

MARIE   Tell me I'll never have to be out there again.

Jess puts his arms around her and holds her.

JESS   You'll never have to be out there again.

They kiss.

CUT TO:

INT. SALLY'S BATHROOM—DAY
Sally looking at herself in the mirror as she puts on makeup.

SALLY   *(Voice-over)*   I'll just say we made a mistake—

CUT TO:

INT. HARRY'S BATHROOM—DAY
Harry is showering.

HARRY   *(Voice-over)*   Sally, it was a mistake—

CUT TO:

INT. SALLY'S BATHROOM—DAY
As before.

SALLY   *(Voice-over)*   I just hope I get to say it first.

CUT TO:

INT. HARRY'S BATHROOM—DAY
Harry still showering.

HARRY   *(Voice-over)*   I hope she says it before I do.

CUT TO:

INT. RESTAURANT—NIGHT
Sally and Harry sit, silently, with their drinks. Long pause.

SALLY   It was a mistake.

HARRY   I'm so relieved that you think so, too.

Both of them take swigs of their water.

HARRY (CONT'D)   I'm not saying last night wasn't great.

SALLY   It was.

HARRY   Yes, it was.

SALLY   We just never should've done it.

HARRY   I couldn't agree more.

Sally nods.

A pause.

SALLY I'm so relieved.

HARRY Great.

SALLY Yeah.

Harry nodding.

Sally nodding.

Well, that's that.

A WAITER brings their salads.

WAITER Two mixed green salads.

They start to eat.

They eat.

Silence.

We hear the FORKS against the plates.

More silence.

HARRY It is so nice when you can sit with someone and not have to talk.

HOLD on the scene as they go on eating in silence.

HOLD.

HOLD.

                                                    CUT TO:

EXT. CENTRAL PARK—BETHESDA FOUNTAIN—DAY
Harry and Jess fast-walking along.

HARRY It's just like, most of the time you go to bed with someone and then she tells you all her stories, you tell her your stories, but with Sally and me we'd already heard each other's stories, so once we went to bed, we didn't know what we were supposed to do, you know?

JESS Sure, Harry.

EXT. STREET—RAINING
Harry and Jess crossing the street.

HARRY   I don't know, you get to a certain point in a relationship where it's just too late to have sex, you know?

CUT TO:

INT. DEPARTMENT STORE FITTING ROOM—DAY
We can see Marie standing at a mirror, Sally in a chair.

SALLY   Is Harry bringing anyone to the wedding?

MARIE   I don't think so.

SALLY   Is he seeing anyone?

MARIE   He was seeing this anthropologist, but . . .

SALLY   What did she look like?

MARIE   Thin. Pretty. Big tits. Your basic nightmare. So what do you think?

Marie is trying on a very traditional white wedding dress with a train and veil.

SALLY   Oh, Marie.

MARIE   Tell me the truth.

Sally's eyes start to well with tears.

SALLY   It's just beautiful.

CUT TO:

INT. WEDDING—AFTERNOON
The wedding. A winter wedding with pine boughs and holly.

Marie in her wedding dress with a gorgeous bouquet of flowers comes down the aisle with her father and Sally, who's the maid of honor.

A chamber MUSIC quartet is playing something by Mozart as they come down the aisle to a JUDGE who's standing at the head of the aisle next to Jess and Harry, his best man.

The ceremony begins. Harry looks at Sally. She looks at him for a moment, then looks away.

JUDGE   We are gathered here today to celebrate the marriage of Marie and Jess and to consecrate their vows of matrimony. The vows they will take will join their lives, the wine they will share binds all their hopes together, and by the rings they will wear, they will be known to all as husband and wife.

CUT TO:

INT. PUCK BUILDING—WEDDING RECEPTION—AFTERNOON
A band is PLAYING.

Harry approaches Sally.

HARRY   Hi.

SALLY   Hello.

HARRY   Nice ceremony.

SALLY   Beautiful.

Sally is clearly uncomfortable. She's going to behave like someone who simply is not going to get involved or even pretend interest in the conversation.

HARRY   Boy, the holidays are rough. Every year I just try to get from the day before Thanksgiving to the day after New Year's.

Sally nods.

SALLY   A lot of suicides.

Harry nods. Sally nods.

A WAITER comes up with a tray of hors d'oeuvres.

WAITER   Would you like a pea pod with shrimp?

SALLY   *(with all the warmth she hasn't been showing Harry)*   Thank you.

She takes one. Waiter turns the tray to Harry.

HARRY   No thanks.

The Waiter leaves.

HARRY   How've you been?

SALLY   Fine.

A pause.

HARRY   Are you seeing anybody?

Sally looks at him.

SALLY   Harry—

HARRY   What?

SALLY   *(cutting him off)*   I don't want to talk about this.

HARRY   Why not?

SALLY   I don't want to talk about it.

Sally turns and walks away. Harry follows.

HARRY   Why can't we get past this? I mean, are we gonna carry this thing around forever?

Sally stops, whirls around to face him.

SALLY   Forever? It just happened.

HARRY   It happened three weeks ago.

Sally looks at him disbelievingly.

HARRY (CONT'D)   You know how a year to a person is like seven years to a dog?

SALLY   Yes.

Harry throws up his hands as if it's self-explanatory.

SALLY (CONT'D)   Is one of us supposed to be a dog in this scenario?

HARRY   Yes.

SALLY   Who is the dog?

HARRY   You are.

SALLY   I am? I'm the dog?

HARRY   Um-hmm.

SALLY   I am the dog?

People are starting to notice the intensity of the conversation.

Sally is really furious now. She starts toward the large doors in the background, thinking they can get some privacy there. Once in front of the doors, she stands angrily with her hands on her hips, away from the guests.

SALLY (CONT'D)   I don't see that, Harry. If anybody is the dog, you are the dog. You want to act like what happened didn't mean anything.

HARRY   I'm not saying it didn't mean anything. I'm saying why does it have to mean *everything*?

SALLY   Because it does, and you should know that better than anyone because the minute that it happened, you walked right out the door.

HARRY   I didn't walk out—

SALLY   No, sprinted is more like it.

HARRY   We both agreed it was a mistake—

SALLY   The worst mistake I ever made.

INT. KITCHEN—DAY

They go through the doors Sally was heading for and now they're in the kitchen. Waiters are banging by with trays, dumping glasses into the sink, opening champagne, etc. Harry and Sally shouting now over the DIN.

HARRY   What do you want from me?

SALLY   I don't want anything from you.

HARRY   Fine, fine, but let's just get one thing straight. I didn't go over there that night to make love to you. That's not why I went there. But you looked at me with those big, weepy eyes. "Don't go home tonight, Harry. Hold me a little longer, Harry." What was I supposed to do?

SALLY   What are you saying? You took pity on me?

HARRY   No, I . . .

SALLY   Fuck you!

Sally slaps Harry across the face. Then bursts out of the kitchen with a stunned Harry right behind her.

INT. PUCK BUILDING—WEDDING RECEPTION—DAY
The entire wedding party is assembled around the bandstand.

The band is PLAYING some kind of musical riff that signals that attention must be paid. Sally stomps through the room, Harry just behind. There's a crowd of guests assembled in a knot with Jess and Marie, their arms around each other, standing there with their champagne glasses. Jess is in front of the microphone.

JESS   Everybody, could I have your attention, please? I want to propose a toast to Harry and Sally.

Sally, surprised, comes to a halt, as does Harry. The entire crowd turns toward the two of them.

JESS (CONT'D)   If Marie or I had found either of them remotely attractive, we would not be here today.

Everyone laughs and raises their glasses to Harry and Sally.

FADE OUT.

MUSIC HERE

FADE IN:

EXT. 96TH STREET—CHRISTMAS TREE STAND—DAY
Sally, in jeans and a plain jacket, has just bought her Christmas tree, and the salesman has finished putting plastic netting around it. Sally starts to carry the tree. It's very heavy; the top of it is dragging slightly behind her, and she's leaving a little trail of pine needles behind her

as she starts home, but she's going to carry this damn tree home alone if it kills her.

CUT TO:

INT. HARRY'S APARTMENT—DAY
Harry paces in the kitchen, the phone to his ear, as he makes a cup of tea.

HARRY *(into phone)* Hi, it's me. It's the holiday season, and I thought I might remind you that this is the season of charity and forgiveness . . .

INT. SALLY'S APARTMENT—DAY
Sally brings in the tree.

HARRY'S VOICE (CONT'D) *(on answering machine)* . . . and although it's not widely known, it's also the season of groveling. So if you felt like calling me back, I'd be all too happy to do the traditional Christmas grovel. Give me a call.

INT. HARRY'S APARTMENT—DAY
Harry at the counter, hangs up, carries his cup to the table, sits, and looks through his mail.

CUT TO:

INT. SALLY'S APARTMENT—DAY
Sally works at her computer. The phone RINGS. She stops working and listens to the answering machine.

SALLY'S VOICE *(on answering machine)* Hi, I'm not home right now. Call you right back.

Machine BEEPS.

HARRY'S VOICE *(on answering machine)* If you're there, please pick up the phone. I really want to talk to you.

INT. HARRY'S APARTMENT—DAY
Harry is lying on his bed, talking on the phone.

HARRY (CONT'D) The fact that you're not answering

leads me to believe you're either (a) not at home, (b) home but don't want to talk to me, or (c) . . .

> INT. SALLY'S APARTMENT—DAY
> *Sally, not picking up.*

HARRY'S VOICE (CONT'D) *(on answering machine)* . . . home, desperately want to talk to me but trapped under something heavy. If it's (a) or (c), call me back.

> *The phone CLICKS off. HOLD on Sally.*

> > > > CUT TO:

> EXT. STREET—HOT DOG STAND—DAY
> *Harry and Jess are stopped at a hot dog stand.*

HARRY Obviously she doesn't want to talk to me. What do I have to do? Get hit over the head? If she wants to call me, she'll call me. I'm through making a schmuck out of myself.

> > > > CUT TO:

> INT. HARRY'S APARTMENT—DAY
> *Harry singing on the phone. The backup MUSIC machine is going.*

HARRY *(singing)* "If you're feeling sad and lonely, There's a service I can render . . .

> INT. SALLY'S APARTMENT—DAY
> *Sally is getting ready to leave. She glances at her machine as she hears:*

HARRY'S VOICE (CONT'D) *(singing, on answering machine)* ". . . Tell the one who digs you only, I can be so warm and tender—Call me, maybe it's late but just Call me . . ."

> INT. HARRY'S APARTMENT—DAY

HARRY (CONT'D) *(singing into the phone)* "Don't be afraid to just Phone moi . . ."

> INT. SALLY'S APARTMENT—DAY

HARRY'S VOICE (CONT'D) *(singing, on answering machine)* "Call me and I'll be around."

Sally just stares.

INT. HARRY'S APARTMENT—DAY

HARRY (CONT'D) *(into phone, speaking)* Give me a call.

He switches off the song machine.

SALLY *(through filter)* Hi, Harry.

INT. HARRY'S APARTMENT—DAY

HARRY Hello! Hi, hi! I didn't think that you would . . . that you were there.

INT. SALLY'S APARTMENT—DAY

HARRY *(through filter)* What are you doing?

SALLY I was just on my way out.

HARRY *(through filter)* Where are you going?

SALLY What do you want, Harry?

INT. HARRY'S APARTMENT—DAY

HARRY Nothing. Nothing, I just called to say I'm sorry.

INT. SALLY'S APARTMENT—DAY

SALLY Okay.

She waits for him to seize the moment. Which he doesn't.

INT. HARRY'S APARTMENT—DAY
He doesn't know what else to say.

INT. SALLY'S APARTMENT—DAY

SALLY I gotta go.

INT. HARRY'S APARTMENT—DAY

HARRY Wait a second . . . wait a second. What are

you doing for New Year's? Are you going to the
Tylers' party? 'Cause I don't have a date, and if you
don't have a date, we always said that if neither one
of us had a date . . .

INT. SALLY'S APARTMENT—DAY

HARRY *(through filter)* . . . we could be together for
New Year's, and . . .

SALLY Harry, I can't do this anymore. I am not your
consolation prize. Goodbye.

She hangs up.

INT. HARRY'S APARTMENT—DAY
Harry stands there, listening to the DIAL TONE.

FADE OUT.

FADE IN:

INT. HARRY'S APARTMENT—NIGHT
A tight shot, on television, of DICK CLARK.

DICK CLARK *(on television)* And here we are, once again,
the sixteenth annual New Year's Rockin' Eve, coming
to you live from the heart . . .

We PULL BACK TO REVEAL

*Harry lying in bed eating Mallomars and watching Dick Clark on
television.*

HARRY *(Voice-over)* What's so bad about this? You
have Dick Clark, that's tradition, you have Mallomars,
the greatest cookie of all time, and you're about to
give the Knicks their first championship since 1973.

Harry aims a toy basketball at a plastic basket mounted on the wall.

He misses.

He looks back at the television set.

CUT TO:

INT. NEW YEAR'S EVE PARTY—NIGHT
A great big New Year's Eve party, just like the one we were at a year earlier. The mirrored ball is twirling. Twinkly lights on everyone's face.

Sally dancing with a tall man. He dips her. She's appalled. Upright again, she catches Marie's eye as the tall man swoops her about the floor. Marie is dancing with Jess.

SALLY   I don't know why I let you drag me to this.

And she's yanked out of frame.

CUT TO:

EXT. STREET—STOREFRONTS—NIGHT
Harry walks along an empty street.

EXT. DOWNTOWN STREET—NIGHT
Harry walking down the street past shop windows.

HARRY   *(Voice-over)*   This is much better. Fresh air. I have the streets all to myself. Who needs to be at a big, crowded party pretending to have a good time? Plus this is the perfect time to catch up on my window shopping. This is good.

He sees a couple across the street standing with their arms around each other in front of a store window. The woman laughs.

CUT TO:

INT. NEW YEAR'S EVE PARTY—NIGHT
Sally is leaning against a pillar facing a MAN AT THE PARTY, who is telling her a joke.

MAN AT THE PARTY   So the guy says, "Read the card."

Sally leans around the pillar toward Marie, who's on the other side.

SALLY (CONT'D)   I'm going home.

MARIE   You'll never get a taxi.

CUT TO:

EXT. WASHINGTON SQUARE—NIGHT
Harry is walking along the same place he was dropped off by Sally
eleven years ago. He has an ice-cream cone. He dumps the ice cream
in a trash can. He stops and looks up at the Washington Square Arch.

HARRY *(Voice-over Flashback)*   You realize, of course, that
we could never be friends.

FLASHBACK—DAY
At the Square under the Arch, Sally and Harry are at the back of her
car, facing each other. Sally extends her hand to Harry.

SALLY *(Voice-over Flashback)*   Why not?

Harry shakes Sally's hand.

HARRY *(Voice-over Flashback)*   What I'm saying . . . is
that men and women . . .

FLASHBACK—DAY
Sally and Harry in the airplane.

HARRY *(Voice-over Flashback)* (CONT'D)   . . . can't be
friends, because the sex part always gets in the way.

FLASHBACK—DAY
Harry and Sally walking down the street.

SALLY *(Voice-over Flashback)*   That's not true.

HARRY *(Voice-over Flashback)*   No man can be friends
with . . .

FLASHBACK—DAY
Harry and Sally walking in the park.

HARRY *(Voice-over Flashback)* (CONT'D)   . . . a woman he
finds attractive. He always wants to have sex with
her.

FLASHBACK—DAY
Harry and Sally in the museum—she is laughing.

SALLY   *(Voice-over Flashback)*   What if *they* don't want to have sex with *you*?

HARRY   *(Voice-over Flashback)*   Doesn't matter . . .

FLASHBACK—DAY
Harry and Sally in deli, when Sally is faking an orgasm as other customers look on.

HARRY   *(Voice-over Flashback)* (CONT'D)   . . . because the sex thing is already out there, so the friendship is ultimately doomed . . .

FLASHBACK—NIGHT
Harry and Sally kissing in her bedroom.

HARRY   *(Voice-over Flashback)* (CONT'D)   . . . and that is the end of the story.

SALLY   *(Voice-over Flashback)*   Well, I guess we're not going to be friends, then.

HARRY   *(Voice-over Flashback)*   Guess not.

SALLY   *(Voice-over Flashback)*   That's too bad. You were the only person I knew in New York.

EXT. WASHINGTON SQUARE—NIGHT
Harry back in reality. Thinking about what just happened in his mind. He feels the cold and turns his collar up, then starts walking slowly away from the Arch. We stay with Harry as his pace starts to quicken and finally ends with him running down the street.

                                        CUT TO:

INT. NEW YEAR'S EVE PARTY—NIGHT
It's almost midnight. Balloons, confetti, the mirrored ball spinning slowly around.

The excitement in the room builds as we approach midnight. We see Sally standing alone in the crowd.

She decides to leave. She makes her way to Jess and Marie.

CUT TO:

EXT. STREET—NIGHT
Harry running.

CUT TO:

INT. NEW YEAR'S EVE PARTY—NIGHT

SALLY *(going for her coat)* I'm going.

MARIE It's almost midnight.

SALLY The thought of not kissing somebody is just . . .

JESS I'll kiss you.

CUT TO:

EXT. STREET—NIGHT
Harry is looking for a cab. He can't find one. He keeps running.

CUT TO:

INT. NEW YEAR'S EVE PARTY—NIGHT

JESS C'mon, stay. Please.

SALLY Thanks, Jess. I just . . . I have to go.

MARIE Oh, wait two minutes.

SALLY I'll call you tomorrow.

They kiss each other on the cheek, and Sally heads off.

CUT TO:

EXT. STREET—NIGHT
Harry runs along the street, rounds the corner, and runs into the hotel and through the lobby.

CUT TO:

INT. NEW YEAR'S EVE PARTY—NIGHT
Sally is making her way through the crowd when she stops dead in her tracks. It's Harry. Slowly he comes toward her and stops in front of her.

HARRY I've been doing a lot of thinking. And the thing is, I love you.

SALLY What?

HARRY I love you.

SALLY How do you expect me to respond to this?

HARRY How about you love me, too?

SALLY How about, I'm leaving.

Sally turns and walks off, parting the crowd. Harry follows her like a terrier.

HARRY Doesn't what I said mean anything to you?

Sally stops and turns to face him. During the following, we hear the COUNTDOWN to the New Year, after which everyone breaks into "HAPPY NEW YEAR," confetti flies, everyone is kissing and breaking into "AULD LANG SYNE."

SALLY I'm sorry, Harry. I know it's New Year's Eve, and I know you're feeling lonely, but you just can't show up here, tell me you love me, and expect to make everything all right. It doesn't work that way.

HARRY Well, how does it work?

SALLY I don't know, but not this way.

Sally turns to go, but Harry grabs her, stopping her.

HARRY How about this way? I love how you get cold when it's seventy-one degrees out. I love that it takes you an hour and a half to order a sandwich. I love that you get a little crinkle right there when you're looking at me like I'm nuts. I love that after I spend the day with you, I can still smell your perfume on my clothes. And I love that you're the last person I want to talk to before I go to sleep at night. And it's not because I'm lonely. And it's not because it's New

Year's Eve. I came here tonight because when you realize you want to spend the rest of your life with somebody, you want the rest of your life to start as soon as possible.

SALLY *(furious)* That is just like you, Harry. You say things like that, and you make it impossible for me to hate you, and I hate you, Harry. I really hate you. I hate you.

Harry puts his arms around her.

They kiss.

A long kiss.

The twinkle ball goes around, twinkling.

They go on kissing.

"AULD LANG SYNE" continues in the background.

HARRY What does this song mean? My whole life, I have never known what this song means. I mean, "Should old acquaintance be forgot"? Does that mean we should forget old acquaintances, or does it mean if we happened to forget them, we should remember them, which is not possible because we already forgot them?

SALLY Well, maybe it just means that we should remember that we forgot them or something. Anyway, it's about old friends.

They start to kiss again.

And as the camera PULLS UP away from them:

HARRY *(Voice-over)* The first time we met we hated each other.

SALLY *(Voice-over)* You didn't hate me, I hated you. *(beat)* And the second time we met, you didn't even remember me.

HARRY *(Voice-over)* I did too, I remembered you. *(a long beat)* The third time we met, we became friends.

SALLY *(Voice-over)* We were friends for a long time.

HARRY *(Voice-over)* And then we weren't.

SALLY *(Voice-over)* And then we fell in love.

CUT TO:

A COUPLE ON A LOVE SEAT
HARRY and SALLY together.

SALLY Three months later we got married.

HARRY It only took three months.

SALLY Twelve years and three months.

HARRY We had this . . . really wonderful wedding.

SALLY It really was.

HARRY It was great. We had this enormous coconut cake.

SALLY Huge coconut cake with the tiers, and there was this very rich chocolate sauce on the side.

HARRY Right. Because not everybody likes it on the cake, because it makes it very soggy.

SALLY Particularly coconut. It soaks up a lot of that stuff. It's important to keep it on the side.

HARRY Right . . .

And as they continue on, we—

FADE OUT.

THE END

A NOTE ON THE TYPE

The text of this book was set by CRT in Compano,
a film version of Palatino, a type face designed by the noted
German typographer Hermann Zapf. Named
after Giovanbattista Palatino,
a writing master of Renaissance Italy, Palatino was the first
of Zapf's type faces to be introduced in America. The first
designs for the face were made in 1948, and the
fonts for the complete face were issued between 1950 and
1952. Like all Zapf-designed type faces, Palatino
is beautifully balanced and
exceedingly readable.

Composed by The Haddon Craftsmen, Inc.,
Scranton, Pennsylvania
Printed and bound by Fairfield Graphics,
Fairfield, Pennsylvania